大學語文

**A PRIMER FOR ADVANCED BEGINNERS
OF CHINESE VOLUME ONE**

This chart shows the evolution of Chinese characters from the earliest style to the current standard style; the characters are, from right to left: moon, horse, fish, peace, and bright. The evolution of styles is shown vertically from top to bottom as: Oracle Bone style, Great Script style, Clerical style, Standard Script style, and Draft style.

FRONTISPIECE DESIGNED BY HAILONG WANG

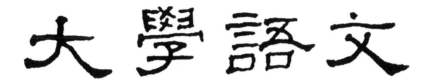

A PRIMER FOR ADVANCED BEGINNERS
OF CHINESE VOLUME ONE

Duanduan Li, Irene Liu, Lening Liu,
Hailong Wang, Zhirong Wang, and Yanping Xie

EDITED BY Irene Liu and Hailong Wang

COLUMBIA UNIVERSITY PRESS / NEW YORK

COLUMBIA UNIVERSITY PRESS
Publishers Since 1893
New York   Chichester, West Sussex
Copyright © 2003 Columbia University Press
All rights reserved

Library of Congress Cataloging-in-Publication Data

A primer for advanced beginners of Chinese = [Da xue yu wen]/Duanduan Li . . . [et al];
edited by Irene Liu and Hailong Wang.

p. cm.
Parallel title in Chinese character.
ISBN 0-231-12383-3 (set : pbk. : alk. paper) — ISBN 978-0-231-12555-0 (v. 1 : pbk. : alk. paper)
— ISBN 0-231-12557-7 (v. 2 : pbk. : alk. paper)
1. Chinese language—Textbooks for foreign speakers—English. I. Title: Da xue yu wen.
II. Li, Duanduan. III. Liu, Ruinian. IV. Wang, Hailong.
PL1129.E5 P73 2001
495.1'82421—dc21

Columbia University Press books
are printed on permanent and durable acid-free paper.
Printed in the United States of America
p 10 9 8 7 6 5

目錄
CONTENTS

前言	*Preface*	xi
鳴謝	*Acknowledgements*	xv
縮略語表	*List of Abbreviations*	xvii
導論	*Introduction: The Basics of Pronunciation and Characters*	xix
	發音、漢字	

第一課　中國人的姓名　　　　　　　　　　　　　　　　　　1
Lesson 1　Chinese Names

生詞	Vocabulary	2
課文	Text	6
閱讀訓練	Reading Skills	7
會話	Dialogue	8
語法	Grammatical Points	10
	Topic-Comment Sentence	10
	Fixed Adverbs：不、也、很、都	10
	Question Particles：嗎、呢、吧	10
	Modifier Particle：的	11
句型和詞匯用法	Sentence Patterns and Word Usage	13
練習	Exercises	15
語音練習	Pronunciation	15
漢字練習	Chinese Characters	15
詞匯練習	Vocabulary Practice	17
語法練習	Grammar	17
寫作練習	Writing	18
閱讀練習	Reading Comprehension	18
日常話題詞匯	Words and Expressions on Specific Topics:	20
課堂用語	Expressions Used in Class	

第二課　中國人的家庭　　　　　　　　　　　　　　　　　　21
Lesson 2　Chinese Families

生詞	Vocabulary	22
課文	Text	26

閱讀訓練 Reading Skills	27
會話 Dialogues	28
語法 Grammatical Points	30
Numbers	30
Measure Words	30
Noun Phrases	31
Coverbs	31
句型和詞匯用法 Sentence Patterns and Word Usage	32
練習 Exercises	33
語音練習 Pronunciation	33
漢字練習 Chinese Characters	33
詞匯練習 Vocabulary Practice	34
語法練習 Grammar	35
綜合練習 Comprehensive Exercises	36
口語練習 Oral Exercise	37
寫作練習 Writing	37
閱讀練習 Reading Comprehension	37
日常話題詞匯 Words and Expressions on Specific Topics: 錢 Money	38

第三課 大江南北
Lesson 3 China: The North and the South   39

生詞 Vocabulary	40
課文 Text	43
閱讀訓練 Reading Skills	44
會話 Dialogue	45
語法 Grammatical Points	47
Place Words	47
Type of Place Words	47
Use of Place Words	48
句型和詞匯用法 Sentence Patterns and Word Usage	50
練習 Exercises	51
語音練習 Pronunciation	51
漢字練習 Chinese Characters	51
詞匯練習 Vocabulary Practice	52
語法練習 Grammar	53
口語練習 Oral Exercise	54
寫作練習 Writing	54
閱讀練習 Reading Comprehension	54
日常話題詞匯 Words and Expressions on Specific Topics: 方位 Locations	56

第四課　十個太陽　　　　　　　　　　　　　　　　57
Lesson 4　The Ten Suns

 生詞　Vocabulary　　　　　　　　　　　　　　　58
 課文　Text　　　　　　　　　　　　　　　　　　61
 閱讀訓練　Reading Skills　　　　　　　　　　　63
 會話　Dialogues　　　　　　　　　　　　　　　64
 語法　Grammatical Points　　　　　　　　　　　66
  The Functions of *le* (了)　　　　　　　　　　66
   Sentence-Final *le* (Sentence-*le*)　　　　　66
   Verb Suffix *le* (Verb-*le*)　　　　　　　　66
   Combination of Verb-*le* and Sentence-*le*　67
   Time Elapsed Without Doing Something　　67
   Situations When V-*le* Is Not Used　　　　68
 句型和詞匯用法　Sentence Patterns and Word Usage　70
 練習　Exercises　　　　　　　　　　　　　　　73
  語音漢字練習　Pronunciation and Characters　73
  詞匯練習　Vocabulary Practice　　　　　　74
  語法練習　Grammar　　　　　　　　　　　75
  綜合練習　Comprehensive Exercises　　　　76
  寫作練習　Writing　　　　　　　　　　　　77
  閱讀練習　Reading Comprehension　　　　78
 日常話題詞匯　Words and Expressions on Specific Topics:　79
 時間　Time

第五課　天和地　　　　　　　　　　　　　　　　81
Lesson 5　Heaven and Earth

 生詞　Vocabulary　　　　　　　　　　　　　　　82
 課文　Text　　　　　　　　　　　　　　　　　　84
 閱讀訓練　Reading Skills　　　　　　　　　　　86
 會話　Dialogue　　　　　　　　　　　　　　　88
 語法　Grammatical Points　　　　　　　　　　　89
  The Use of *le* in Discourse　　　　　　　　89
  Action Verb and Complements of Result　　90
   Actual Type　　　　　　　　　　　　90
   Potential Type　　　　　　　　　　　91
 句型和詞匯用法　Sentence Patterns and Word Usage　92
 練習　Exercises
  語音漢字練習　Pronunciation and Characters　93
  詞匯語法練習　Vocabulary and Grammar　　94
  綜合練習　Comprehensive Exercises　　　　95
  口語練習　Oral Exercise　　　　　　　　　96
  寫作練習　Writing　　　　　　　　　　　　96

閱讀練習 Reading Comprehension		96
日常話題詞匯 Words and Expressions on Specific Topics: 天氣 Weather		98

第六課　成語故事
Lesson 6　The Story of Chinese Idioms
99

生詞 Vocabulary		100
課文 Text		103
閱讀訓練 Reading Skills		105
會話 Dialogue		107
語法 Grammatical Points		108
The Particle "得"		108
句型和詞匯用法 Sentence Patterns and Word Usage		109
練習 Exercises		111
語音練習 Pronunciation		111
漢字練習 Chinese Characters		111
詞匯練習 Vocabulary Practice		112
語法練習 Grammar		114
寫作練習 Writing		114
閱讀練習 Reading Comprehension		114
日常話題詞匯 Words and Expressions on Specific Topics: 常用量詞 Commonly Used Measure Words		117

第七課　萬里長城
Lesson 7　The Great Wall
119

生詞 Vocabulary		120
課文 Text		123
閱讀訓練 Reading Skills		126
會話 Dialogue		128
語法 Grammatical Points		130
Directional Complement (DC)		130
Actual Type of DC		130
Potential Type of DC		131
句型和詞匯用法 Sentence Patterns and Word Usage		132
練習 Exercises		134
語音練習 Pronunciation		134
漢字練習 Chinese Characters		134
詞匯練習 Vocabulary Practice		135
語法練習 Grammar		136
綜合練習 Comprehensive Exercises		138
寫作練習 Writing		139

閱讀練習	Reading Comprehension	139
日常話題詞匯	Words and Expressions on Specific Topics: 旅行 Travel	142

第八課　李白學習的故事
Lesson 8　Li Bai Learns A Lesson 　145

生詞	Vocabulary	146
課文	Text	149
閱讀訓練	Reading Skills	151
會話	Dialogues	153
語法	Grammatical Points	155
	Sentence Pattern Using "ba" ("把")	155
	When and Why a Speaker Uses the 把 Construction	155
句型和詞匯用法	Sentence Patterns and Word Usage	157
練習	Exercises	159
語音練習	Pronunciation	159
漢字練習	Chinese Characters	159
詞匯語法練習	Vocabulary and Grammar	160
綜合練習	Comprehensive Exercises	161
寫作練習	Writing	162
閱讀練習	Reading Comprehension	162
口語練習	Oral Exercise	163
日常話題詞匯	Words and Expressions on Specific Topics: 校園生活 Campus Life	164

第九課　神農和中藥
Lesson 9　Shen Nong and Chinese Medicine 　167

生詞	Vocabulary	168
課文	Text	171
閱讀訓練	Reading Skills	173
會話	Dialogue	174
語法	Grammatical Points	175
	Sequencing in Chinese Narrative Discourse	175
	Succession of Events and Situations	175
	Simultaneity	176
	Overlap	176
	Aspect Marker "guo" (過)	176
句型和詞匯用法	Sentence Patterns and Word Usage	177
練習	Exercises	178
語音漢字練習	Pronunciation and Characters	178
語法詞匯練習	Grammar and Vocabulary	179

	口語練習	Oral Exercises	180
	寫作練習	Writing	180
	閱讀練習	Reading Comprehension	180
	日常話題詞匯	Words and Expressions on Specific Topics:	182
	問路 Asking for Directions		

第十課　中國菜 183
Lesson 10 Chinese Food 183

生詞	Vocabulary	184
課文	Text	188
閱讀訓練	Reading Skills	190
會話	Dialogue	191
語法	Grammatical Points	193
	The "*shi......de*" Construction (是...的)	193
句型和詞匯用法	Sentence Patterns and Word Usage	195
練習	Exercises	197
語音練習	Pronunciation	197
漢字練習	Chinese Characters	197
詞匯練習	Vocabulary Practice	198
語法練習	Grammar	199
口語練習	Oral Exercises	200
寫作練習	Writing	201
閱讀練習	Reading Comprehension	201
日常話題詞匯	Words and Expressions on Specific Topics:	204
買東西 Shopping		

附錄I *Appendix I* 205
漢字源流簡論
A Brief History of the Creation of Chinese Characters and the Evolution of the Chinese Writing System

附錄II *Appendix II* 209
詞匯表
Comprehensive Vocabulary List
  English-Chinese 209
  Chinese-English 229

附錄III *Appendix III* 249
單字筆順表
Character Stroke Order

Preface

This book is written for advanced beginners of Chinese. By "advanced beginners," we mean those who can communicate in Chinese orally on subjects like daily routines, although with grammatical mistakes and nonstandard pronunciation, but cannot read or write. They have had some exposure to Chinese popular culture, and they know some Chinese social conventions.

Rationale

The enrollment of "advanced beginners" of Chinese has increased continuously since the early 1990s in the Chinese language programs at many universities. How to teach these students has become more and more of a challenge. For years, the way many programs have coped with this complexity is to use the same textbook and teaching method as that for teaching "true beginners," but at a faster pace. However, this unilateral approach to teaching two distinct kinds of beginners has proved ineffective over the years. These two groups have different needs and interests. For example, learning the basic survival vocabulary and basic structure is of primary importance for true beginners, but is less necessary for advanced beginners. The content of the textbooks designed for true beginners with topics on basic daily routines often bores advanced beginners.

Aside from teaching methods and content of the material, the learning process of the two groups is also different. Compared with "true beginners," advanced beginners have very uneven language skills. While their ability in speaking and listening comprehension is functionally adequate, their reading and writing ability is very weak. Thus, for these students, the development of reading and writing ability is of the utmost importance. Our experiences in teaching advanced beginners over the years have taught us that they need to read more sophisticated materials than the "true beginners," but lack the skills with which to do so. Therefore, for pedagogical reasons, the textbook and teaching methods for advanced beginners need to be redesigned.

Our solution is twofold: (1) to give students readings that are intellectually stimulating but not beyond their lexical, grammatical, or syntactic understanding; and (2) to teach strategies that make reading easier. The exercises are designed to guide students toward acquiring the skills of good readers.

The Format/Structure of the Text

This textbook puts great emphasis on student self-preparation out of class, reinforced performance in class and class discussion, and guided application of learned skills in further exercises and tasks. In order to help students study the lessons at home, the explanations and instructions in this textbook are written out in detail and in simple language. Linguistic jargon is kept to a minimum.

Because advanced beginners already speak the language, they already know the phonetic and grammatical systems. The aim of the book is to make their innate knowledge explicit. Thus, a different approach is taken from the textbooks generally written for true beginners. In pronunciation, aside from briefly introducing the pinyin system, the book concentrates on practicing sounds (e.g., zh-, ch-, sh-, vs. z-, c-, s-; the neutral tone, etc.) in the exercises. Those sounds are usually problematic for a majority of advanced beginners, who speak dialects other than standard Mandarin. In terms of grammar, the book embraces discourse grammar rather than sentence grammar. Simple sentence patterns are introduced only briefly because they are already familiar to the students. But the book concentrates more on grammar points that are unique to the Chinese language, such as the topic-comment sentence, the *shi . . . de* pattern, verb copying, the topic-chain in extended discourse, and so on.

Since this book aims at teaching active reading, reading strategies are introduced. They include guessing meaning from context, using radicals as a guessing tool, making predictions, learning to accept some uncertainty, making inferences, and text organization. Learning the radicals is emphasized in the first ten lessons. The purpose is to introduce students to a tool for character-recognizing and meaning-guessing, so that (1) the students will not become anxious every time they read something new simply because they encounter words they do not know, (2) the students know that they are making an intelligent guess, not just a random guess, and (3) the ability to guess will allow students to truly process reading rather than decoding word for word. Over the next ten lessons, while still working on the radicals as a guessing tool, students will learn how to use the dictionary effectively. We hope that students will move through the book with a growing sense of confidence and accomplishment as they discover they can find the main ideas and important details, can learn new vocabulary without a dictionary, and read new material without anxiety because of their tolerance of some ambiguities. Moreover, students will feel intellectually challenged by material that engages their intelligence.

Because of the nature of this "culture-based" textbook, there may be some uncommonly used words (e.g., proper names) in some lessons. They are not included in the vocabulary list, but put in the category of "words for special use" outside the main vocabulary, which do not require students' memorization of writing. We have also included a section of "Useful Expressions on Specific Topics" at the end of each of the first ten lessons to provide students with more practical expressions for daily communication.

Lesson Format and Objectives

- Pre-reading discussion: This activity requires students to form predictions about what is to be read by having students discuss the pictures provided about the text and answer the questions in the "Getting Started" section.
- First reading: This exercise is to train students to read quickly and try to get the main idea(s) from the text. The students should understand that they are not expected to be able to get all the details from the text. Instead, they should keep in mind the questions asked in the "Getting Started" section.
- Second reading: This exercise focuses on these reading skills: getting the specific information (i.e., details) and understanding the text structure.
- Dialogue: This section links the subject matter and the vocabulary in this lesson, which is often formal and abstract, to more practical use in daily conversations.
- Grammar explanation: This section introduces important grammatical points that are either unclear or unknown to the students, especially at the discourse level.
- Exercise: The exercises include sound and tone discrimination, the practice of grammar, word usage, guessing meaning by utilizing radicals, using a dictionary, reading skills, and writing.
- Discussion: Students can actively practice their newly learned vocabulary words and reinforce their knowledge learned from the lessons as they express their opinions and share ideas in the discussion section.
- Reading comprehension: This section provides additional reading. Including unfamiliar words in each reading, the material in this section is not too difficult. The purpose is for the students to practice reading quickly and still enjoy it. They will learn how to guess words from context and

to tolerate ambiguity of meaning. The focus of the practice is to get the general meanings of the text.
- When introducing grammar, we provide English translations only for those sentences in which English makes the point clearer.

Acknowledgments

It has been a great working experience for all of us who have cooperated in writing this book in that we have learned how differences of opinions are expressed and how compromise is reached. Every one of us has contributed much of his or her free time to the project. Since 1999, the text has been taught on a trial basis for nine semesters, five in three regular school years and four in the 2000 and 2001 Beijing Columbia summer session. The planning period started with designing and conducting surveys of the advanced beginners in elementary Chinese class at Columbia in 1997, seeking their opinions concerning topics of interest and preference. While writing the book, in addition to frequent consultations with the students, we held two meetings with the students who had used the book at the end of each semester in order to solicit their critical opinions. We also collected the students' written comments on the first versions of the book. Each of these steps, from trial-teaching to the consultations with students, has resulted in our multiple revisions of the text.

We are most grateful to Professor David Wang, chairman of the Department of East Asian Languages and Cultures, for his unfailing support. We also thank Professor John Meskill for editing the English of the whole book. We are indebted to Professor Chauncey Chu for his advice on discourse grammar. Appreciation is due to the three outside reviewers for their positive reviews and suggestions. These suggestions, which we value greatly, have helped us make the textbook better. Finally, we thank all the students who have provided us with their generous and unreserved comments and suggestions.

The authors of the lessons are as follows:

Lesson	Author	Lesson	Author
Lesson 1	Duanduan Li	Lesson 11	Zhirong Wang
Lesson 2	Yanping Xie	Lesson 12	Yanping Xie
Lesson 3	Yanping Xie	Lesson 13	Lening Liu
Lesson 4	Irene Liu	Lesson 14	Yanping Xie
Lesson 5	Irene Liu	Lesson 15	Lening Liu
Lesson 6	Duanduan Li	Lesson 16	Zhirong Wang
Lesson 7	Duanduan Li	Lesson 17	Irene Liu
Lesson 8	Hailong Wang	Lesson 18	Hailong Wang
Lesson 9	Lening Liu	Lesson 19	Hailong Wang
Lesson 10	Zhirong Wang	Lesson 20	Hailong Wang

In addition to the collective effort of each author to the whole project, we acknowledge the contributions of Irene Liu for the general management of the project.

This book was supported in part by a grant from the Consortium for Language Teaching and Learning.

The authors,
Columbia University

縮略語表
Abbreviations

Adv.	……………	adverb
Conj.	……………	conjunction
CV	……………	co-verb
IE	……………	idiomatic expression
Interj.	……………	interjection
Loc.	……………	location
M	……………	measure word
MV	……………	modal verb
N	……………	noun
Nu.	……………	number
Pt.	……………	particle
Pron.	……………	pronoun
Prep.	……………	preposition
PN	……………	proper noun
PW	……………	place word
QW	……………	question word
V	……………	verb
VP	……………	verb phrase
VO	……………	verb-object
SV	……………	stative verb
TW	……………	time word

Introduction: The Basics of Pronunciation and Characters

Pronunciation

This lesson about romanization and pronunciation is a summary of the more difficult and problematic sounds and pinyin symbols. It is intended primarily for students who already know the basic sounds and wish to master romanization.

There are two Chinese names for "Standard Chinese." While *putonghua* (common language) is the term used in mainland China, *guoyu* (national language) is used in Taiwan. For convenience, we will adopt the term *putonghua* throughout the book. The sound system of *putonghua* is that of the Beijing dialect. In the sound system of *putonghua* one syllable corresponds to one character. A syllable is formed by the combination of three components: (1) an initial or beginning sound, (2) a final or the rest of the syllable, and (3) a tone.

Vowels

The basic vowels are: a, o, e, i u, ü.

Initial Sounds

The initial sounds are: b-, p-, m-, f-, d-, t-, n-, l-, g-, k-, h-, j-, q-, x-, zh, ch-, sh-, -r, z-, c-, s-.

Of these twenty-one initial sounds, there are only four that would probably give you trouble, because they are the ones unique to the Beijing dialect. The rest of the initial sounds are already within your grasp. The four sounds—zh-, ch-, sh-, r- —are called retroflex.

They are articulated with the tip of the tongue curled upward and back against or near the juncture of the hard and soft palates.

Final Sounds

The finals or endings are:

A.
-a, -an, -ang, -ai, -ao, -ar
-o, -ou, -ong
-e, -en, -eng, -ei, -er
-i, -in, -ing
-u, -un
-ü, -üe, -üan, -ün

B. The vowels i, u, and ü are special because, like no other vowels, they can go before some endings. When used this way, they are called "medials."

-ia, -iao, -ie, -iu, -ian, -in, -iang, -ing, -iong
-ua, -uo, -uai, -ui, -uan, -un, -uang, -ueng
-üe -üan -ün

C. All syllables with finals beginning with i, u, or ü and no initial sound must be written with y-, w-, or yu-. Compare with B.

ya, yao, ye, yu, yan, yin, yang, ying, yong
wa, wo, wai, wei, wan, wen, wang, weng
yue, yuan, yun

Tones

There are four tones, the first tone " ¯ ", the second tone " ´ ", the third tone " ˇ ", and the fourth tone " ` ". The neutral tone is unique to the Beijing dialect. From the standpoint of single syllables, practically every syllable pronounced alone has one of the four regular tones. But in compounds and connected speech, some syllables become unstressed and lose their characteristic tones, and the pitch is determined, not by the original tones, but by their tonal environment, chiefly by the preceding syllables.

Examples: xǐhuan, míngzi, háizi, xiānsheng, xiūxi

Tone-sandhi

As mentioned above, the tones of syllables spoken in succession are different from those of the same syllables when spoken in isolation. This difference is called tone-sandhi. Tone-sandhi occurs particularly with the third tone.

- A third tone followed by any tone except another third tone is pronounced without its final rising pitch.

Examples: hǎotīng, hǎowán, hǎoshì

- A third tone followed by another third tone changes into the second tone.

Examples: hěnhǎo, fǔdǎo, biǎoyǎn

Mastery of the retroflex and the tones will come with regular practice. It is not enough simply to know the rules. They must be practiced.

Learning Characters

Everyone knows that Chinese characters are difficult to learn, but there are ways to make learning them easier. The following rationale and method will provide you with a means to learn characters more easily and to memorize them better.

A character is a unit of meaning. Most characters have two components: the radical that indicates the general meaning of the character, and the part that usually indicates the general sound category of the character. For example, the characters 江 (river), 湖 (lake), 波 (wave), 沉 (sink), and 灘 (beach) all have the radical 氵 (water). For another example, 説 (speak), 譏 (mock), 論 (comment), 譯 (interpret), and 謠 (rumor) all have the radical 言 (language). As you can see, although there are 50,000 characters, they exist in groups of meaningful categories called radicals. Fortunately there are only 214 radicals and not all of them are in great use. Among these 214 radicals about fifty occur frequently. If you can equip yourself with these 50 radicals, you will have gained the key to learning characters.

Based on the above rationale, the first step in learning a new character is to detect the radical of the character. It takes experience and practice to locate the radical of a character. To start, we offer two common ways to identify the radical of a character. If the character has two or three parts side by side, the left-hand part is most likely the radical of the character. For example, 你、好、湖、做. If the character has an outside enclosure with parts inside, the outside enclosure is the radical. For example, the radical of 國、困、and 圓 is 囗. You will discover the other arrangements between radicals and the components of characters as you progress.

The following are the fifty most frequently used radicals, which you must remember in order to learn characters. Each lesson in this book has an exercise focused on these radicals and learning to use them as a tool to guess the meaning of characters.

I. "Human Being" and Related Group

亻 人 man	手 扌 hand	心 忄 heart	女 女 woman
口 mouth	目 罒 eye	肉 月 flesh	足 𧾷 foot
力 strength	疒 sickness	耳 耳 ear	舌 舌 tone

II. "Animal" Group

| 牛 牜 ox | 犬 犭 dog | 虫 虫 insect | 馬 馬 horse |
| 魚 魚 fish | 鳥 鳥 隹 bird | | |

III. "Action" Group

| 彳 left step | 攵 tap | 辶 run and stop | 食 food, eat |

言 speak

IV. "Nature" Group

土 soil	田 field	禾 grain	竹 bamboo
火 灬 fire	雨 rain	玉 王 jade	山 mountain
石 stone	日 sun	木 wood	米 rice
糸 silk	艹 grass	阝阜 mound	金 gold, metal
水 氵 water			

V. "Manufacturing" Group

| 宀 roof | 广 shelter | 巾 napkin | 刀 刂 knife |
| 衤衣 clothing | 門 door | | |

VI. "Miscellaneous" Group

| 貝 cowries | 大 large | 口 enclosure | 車 vehicle |
| 阝邑 village | 頁 a page | | |

---

xxii   Introduction

大學語文

**A PRIMER FOR ADVANCED BEGINNERS
OF CHINESE** VOLUME ONE

第一課.中國人的姓名

Lesson 1. Chinese Names

Before You Read

Getting Started: This is an ancient text called 百家姓 (Bǎijiāxìng, *The Book of Family Names*), which includes most Chinese family names. Below is the first page from this text. Can you find your family name (or the family names of people you know) on this page?

生詞
VOCABULARY

1.	中國	Zhōngguó	PN	China
2.	人	rén	N	human being; person; people
3.	的	de	Pt.	marker (of noun modifier)
4.	姓	xìng	V/N	one's surname is/surname
5.	名	míng	N	name; given name
6.	前面	qiánmian	L/PW	the front; ahead; preceding
7.	是	shì	V	to be
8.	後面	hòumian	PW/N	back; behind; rear
9.	很	hěn	Adv.	very; quite
10.	多	duō	SV	many; much
11.	常用	chángyòng	SV	commonly used
12.	有	yǒu	V	have; exist; there is/are
13.	一	yī	Nu	one
14.	百	bǎi	Nu	hundred
15.	個	gè	M	general measure word
16.	都	dōu	Adv.	all
17.	來源	láiyuán	N	origin; source
18.	比方說	bǐfāngshuō	IE	for example
19.	以前	yǐqián	TW	before; formerly; previously
20.	地名	dìmíng	N	place name
21.	動物	dòngwù	N	animal
22.	名字	míngzi	N	given name; full name
23.	一定	yídìng	SV/Adv.	certain; certainly; definitely

24.	意思	yìsi	N	meaning
25.	有的	yǒude	Pron.	some
26.	父	fù	N	father
27.	母	mǔ	N	mother
28.	希望	xīwàng	V/N	to hope; hope; to expect; expectation
29.	男	nán	SV	male (as modifier only)
30.	孩	hái	N	child
31.	叫	jiào	V	to call; to name; to be named
32.	女	nǚ	SV	female (as modifier only)
33.	出生	chūshēng	V	to be born
34.	地方	dìfang	N	place; space
35.	北京	Běijīng	PN	Beijing (Peking)
36.	可能	kě'néng	Adv./SV	probably; maybe; possible
37.	美國	Měiguó	PN	America
38.	也	yě	Adv.	too; also; as well; either
39.	時間	shíjiān	N	time
40.	您	nín	Pron.	(respectful, honorific) you
41.	好	hǎo	SV	good; well
42.	請	qǐng	V	please; to invite
43.	問	wèn	V	to ask
44.	貴	guì	SV	(honorific) your; expensive; costly
45.	我	wǒ	Pron.	I; me
46.	呢	ne	Pt.	particle for follow-up questions
47.	吧	ba	Pt.	particle for presuppositions, suggestions, etc.
48.	先生	xiānsheng	N	gentleman; Mr.; husband

49.	小姐	xiǎojie	N	Miss; young lady
50.	甚麼	shénme	QW	what
51.	上海	Shànghǎi	PN	Shanghai
52.	這	zhè/zhèi	Pron.	this
53.	太太	tàitai	N	lady; Mrs.; wife
54.	高興	gāoxìng	SV	happy; glad
55.	認識	rènshi	V	to know; to recognize
56.	你	nǐ	Pron.	you
57.	嗎	ma	Pt.	particle for yes/no questions
58.	不	bù	Adv.	no; not
59.	那	nà/nèi	Pron.	that
60.	位	wèi	M	polite measure word for persons
61.	噢	ō, ò	Interj.	Oh!

Special Vocabulary

Social Conventions

請問	qǐngwèn	IE	May I ask
貴姓	guìxìng	IE	your honorable surname
對不起	duìbuqǐ	IE	I am sorry; Excuse me
沒關係	méi guānxi	IE	It doesn't matter; Never mind
再見	zàijiàn	IE	Good-bye

Family Names/Surnames

張	Zhāng	N	a surname
李	Lǐ	N	a surname
王	Wáng	N	a surname
劉	Liú	N	a surname
趙	Zhào	N	a surname
周	Zhōu	N	a surname
馬	Mǎ	N	horse; a surname
牛	Niú	N	ox; cow; bull; a surname

Words Commonly Used in Given Names

明	míng	SV	bright; brilliant
偉	wěi	SV	great
美	měi	SV/N	beautiful; pretty; abbreviation for America
英	yīng	N	blossom; abbreviation for England
華	huá	N	flower; abbreviation for China
春	chūn	N	spring
秋	qiū	N	autumn

> **First Reading:** Getting the Main Ideas
>
> Quickly read the text and decide which of the three is the *main idea* of this text:
>
> a. 中國人的姓和名字　b. 中國人常用的姓　c. 中國人名字的意思

中國人的姓名

中國人的姓名，前面是姓，後面是名。

中國人的姓很多，常用的姓有一百多個。"張、李、王、劉"都是很常用的姓。中國人的姓有很多來源。比方說，"趙、周"是以前的地名，"馬、牛"都是動物名。

中國人的名字都有一定的意思。有的名字是父母的希望，比方說，男孩叫"明、海"，女孩叫"美、英"。有的名字是一個人出生的地方，比方說，北京出生的孩子可能叫"京生"，美國出生的孩子可能叫"美華"。也有的名字是一個人出生的時間，比方說，"春英"、"秋生"。

Second Reading: Getting the Specific Information

Read the text and fill in the blanks in the following statements with specific information in the text:

1. 中國人的姓名，前面是_____，後面是_____。

2. 中國人常用的姓有_____個。

3. 中國人姓的來源，有的是_____，有的是_____。

4. 中國人的名字，有的是_____，有的是_____，也有的是_____。

Understanding the Text Structure

Write down the topic sentence of each paragraph and list the important points in each paragraph that support the topic sentence.

Paragraph 1. _____

Paragraph 2. _____

　Important points:

　　a. _____

　　b. _____

Paragraph 3. _____

　Important points:

　　a. _____

　　b. _____

　　c. _____

會話
DIALOGUES

（一）

(Mr. and Mrs. Li meet Miss Wang at a party.)

李先生：您好。

王小姐：您好。

李先生：請問您貴姓？

王小姐：我姓王。您呢？

李先生：我姓李，叫京生。

王小姐：李先生一定是北京人吧？

李先生：是啊。請問王小姐是甚麼地方人？

王小姐：我是上海人。

李先生：請問您叫甚麼名字？

王小姐：我叫海英。

李先生：王小姐，這是我太太。

王小姐：李太太，您好。您也是北京人嗎？

李太太：不是，我是美國人。我叫美華。

王小姐：很高興認識你們。

李先生、李太太：認識您我們也很高興。

(二)

(Mr. Wang is looking for a Mr. Li among the guests at a party.)

王：你好！

劉：你好！

王：請問，你是李先生嗎？

劉：我不姓李，我姓劉。那位先生姓李。

王：噢，對不起。

劉：沒關係。

王：再見。

劉：再見。

Practice: Talk with at least five classmates, asking their names, the meaning of their names, where they are from, etc. Give a summary report to the class. Use the following words/phrases: 請問，貴姓，你好，對不起，甚麼地方人，甚麼意思，etc.

語法介紹
GRAMMATICAL POINTS

Topic-Comment Sentence

The word order of general single Chinese sentences is very similar to that of English, i.e., subject-predicate. However, there is a special sentence pattern in Chinese—the topic-comment sentence. The topic of this kind of sentence is usually a person or a thing, but the comment itself consists of a subject-predicate structure. This structure is used very often in Chinese but is not found in European languages. Look at the following examples (the topic of each sentence is underlined):

1. 中國人的姓名，前面是姓，後面是名。
2. 中國人的名字，有的是父母的希望，有的是一個人出生的地方，也有的是一個人出生的時間。
3. 中國地方很大，人也很多。
4. 王太太人很好。
5. 這個人我不認識，你認識嗎?

Fixed Adverbs

不、也、很、都 are adverbs that normally appear right before verbs (or stative verbs). They cannot be put before the subjects or at the end of the sentence. They are also called "non-movable" adverbs. For example:

1. "張、李、王、劉"都是很常用的姓。
2. 認識您我也很高興。
3. 她也姓李。
4. 我不是李先生。

Question Particles 嗎、呢、吧

嗎 is used to turn a statement into a yes/no question. For example:

她先生也是中國人。→ 她先生也是中國人嗎?

Note: This kind of question is the same as the "choice type" question:

她先生是中國人嗎？ = 她先生是不是中國人？

呢 often follows a noun, a pronoun or a phrase to form a follow-up question. What is being asked refers to what was being discussed immediately beforehand. For example:

我姓王。您呢？

您是美國人。您太太呢？

吧 is used to indicate tentativeness of a supposition, suggestion or question.

李先生一定是北京人吧？

我不知道，你問他吧。

Modifier Particle 的

的 links a noun and its modifier. The part after 的 is the head-noun, i.e., what is being talked about. The part before 的 is the modifier, which gives additional information about the head-noun. Pronouns, nouns, stative verbs, verbs, phrases, and clauses can all be used as noun modifiers. The structure is "modifier 的 head-noun." Study the following examples and pay special attention to the difference between the word order in Chinese and English with regard to a modified noun phrase:

1. 中國人的姓名　　(noun 的 head-noun)　　Chinese people's names
2. 她的名字　　(pronoun 的 head-noun)　　her name
3. 常用的姓　　(stative verb 的 head-noun)　　common surnames
4. 北京出生的孩子　　(verbal phrase 的 head-noun)　　children born in Beijing
5. 一個人出生的地方 (clause 的 head-noun)　　the place (where) one was born

Note 1: There are some situations when *de* is not needed:

a) when personal pronouns modify words denoting people closely related to them;

　　e.g., 您(x)太太； 我(x)先生

b) when the modifier is the name of a language, a country, or a city indicating place of origin;

　　e.g., 中國(x)人； 北京(x)人

c) when monosyllabic stative verbs "fuse" with the modified nouns;

e.g., 男(x)孩；女(x)孩；好(x)地方；偉(x)人；貴(x)姓

d) However, when the monosyllabic stative verb is modified by an adverb, *de* is needed, e.g., 好人→ 很好的人

Note 2: When one modifier that takes *de* is added to another modifier that takes *de*, normally only the final *de* is retained; e.g.,

中國人的姓名→ 中國人(x)姓名的來源

孩子的父母 → 孩子(x)父母的希望

句型和詞彙用法
SENTENCE PATTERNS AND WORD USAGE

Study the following examples and create a sentence using each phrase or pattern.

......，有的......，有的......

1. 中國人的姓，有的是以前的地名，有的是動物名。
2. 中國人的名字，有的是父母的希望，有的是一個人出生的地方。
3. 我的朋友，有的是美國人，有的是中國人。
4. 美國人，有的_____，有的_____。

比方說

1. 中國人的姓有很多來源。比方說，"趙、周"是地名，"馬、牛"是動物名。
2. 名字可能是一個人出生的地方。比方說，北京生的人可能就叫"京生"。
3. _____。

以前

1. "趙、周"是以前的地名，"馬、牛"都是動物名。
2. 我以前不認識他。
3. 他父母以前是中國人。
4. _____。

一定

1. 中國人的名字都有一定的意思。
2. 李先生一定是北京人吧？
3. 你一定不認識她吧？她是王小姐。
4. _____。

意思

1. 中國人的名字都有一定的意思。

Lesson 1. Chinese Names

2. 你的名字是甚麽意思?
3. 請問,"希望"是甚麽意思?
4. _____。

可能

1. 北京出生的孩子可能叫"京生"。
2. 他可能不是李先生。
3. 她叫"海英",可能是上海人。
4. _____。

練習
EXERCISES

語音練習 Pronunciation

1. Write the pinyin romanization for the following underlined characters, paying special attention to the difference between the sounds zh/z, sh/s, and ch/c.

<u>中</u>國	姓<u>趙</u>	小<u>周</u>	<u>這</u>個
孩<u>子</u>	名<u>字</u>	<u>再</u>見	意<u>思</u>
不<u>是</u>	比方<u>說</u>	<u>時</u>間	<u>出</u>生
<u>甚</u>麼	<u>上</u>海	<u>春</u>英	<u>當</u>用

2. Write the characters for the following, paying special attention to the underlined syllables:

<u>xī</u>wàng	<u>yǐ</u>qián	hěn<u>duō</u>	Běi<u>jīng</u>
rèn<u>shi</u>	<u>yī</u>	<u>dōu</u>hǎo	<u>qǐng</u>wèn
<u>hěn</u>hǎo	<u>yì</u>bǎi	<u>bú</u>shi	guì<u>xìng</u>
kě<u>néng</u>	<u>yí</u>dìng	<u>bù</u>hǎo	<u>nín</u>hǎo

漢字練習 Chinese Characters

1. Indicate the radical of the following characters, and look up their meaning.

   1). 你　們　個　位　　(部首：＿＿，意思：＿＿＿＿＿＿)

   2). 姓　姐　她　　　(部首：＿＿，意思：＿＿＿＿＿＿)

   3). 時　間　　　　　(部首：＿＿，意思：＿＿＿＿＿＿)

2. Considering the meaning of the radicals, guess the meaning of the following words.

Lesson 1. Chinese Names   15

Match the letter to the character. (Do not use a dictionary.)

佬 _____   a. dawn; daybreak

姥 _____   b. humanity; benevolence

媽 _____   c. heat; hot weather

旦 _____   d. (maternal)grandma

仁 _____   e. mother

暑 _____   f. old man; guy; fellow

3. Which other characters have the same radicals as the words above?

_____

4. Do you know any people who have the following Chinese surnames? Please circle them.

趙 Zhào	錢 Qián	孫 Sūn	李 Lǐ
周 Zhōu	吳 Wú	鄭 Zhèng	王 Wáng
張 Zhāng	陳 Chén	劉 Liú	謝 Xiè
蔣 Jiǎng	沈 Shěn	韓 Hán	楊 Yáng

5. Which of the following names are for females (F) and which are for males (M)? (The English meaning of the given names is provided.)

(   )周美華 (beautiful, flourishing)   (   )劉春林 (spring, forest)

(   )李靜芳 (quiet, fragrant)   (   )趙志強 (aspiration, strong)

(   )王蘭 (orchid)   (   )馬曉東 (dawn, east)

(   )張海琳 (ocean, fine jade)   (   )李京生 (short for Beijing, born)

詞彙練習 Vocabulary Practice

1. 選擇填空 (Fill in the blank with the appropriate word.)

1) 王先生是美國人。我____是美國人。　　a. 都　b. 不　c. 很

2) 張先生是上海人。張太太____是上海人。a. 也　b. 都　c. 有

3) 美國人的名字____有一定的意思嗎？　　a. 不　b. 都　c. 很

4) 我父母是中國人。你父母____？　　　　a. 嗎　b. 吧　c. 呢

5) 你叫京生，一定是北京人____？　　　　a. 嗎　b. 吧　c. 呢

6) A: 請問，您貴姓？B: 我___王，___海英。a. 姓/叫　b. 叫/姓　c. 姓/是

7) A: 認識您很高興。B: 認識您我____高興。a. 都也　b. 很也　c. 也很

8) 美國人的名字，___面是姓，___面是名。a. 前/後　b. 後/前　c. 以前/以後

2. 選詞填空 (Fill in the blanks of the following passage by selecting appropriate words from the list provided.)

(意思、常用、很多、比方說、來源、希望、地方、一定、有的、有的)

中國有_____人，中國人的姓都有一定的_____，中國人的名字也都有_____的意思。_____，_____名字是父母的_____，_____名字是一個人出生的_____。美國也有很多人。Mary, John都是美國人_____的名字。美國人的姓也有來源嗎？美國人的名字也有一定的_____嗎？

語法練習 Grammar

1. Translate the following phrases into Chinese, paying special attention to the word order.

1) <u>my</u> husband _____　　6) <u>Chinese</u> people _____

2) <u>my</u> name _____

3) <u>Mr. Wang's</u> wife _____

4) <u>his</u> wife _____

5) <u>happy</u> people _____

7) <u>good</u> place _____

8) <u>great</u> person _____

9) children <u>born in America</u> _____

10) the place <u>one is born</u> _____

2. Complete the following dialogue.

王: 您好!

李: 您好! _____?

王: 我姓王。_____?

李: 我姓李。

王: _____?

李: 我叫海英。

王: _____?

李: 我是北京人。_____?

王: 我是上海人。

寫作練習 Writing

1. Write your Chinese name and ask your parents about its meaning.

2. Ask your classmates (at least three) their Chinese names and what they mean. Write a short passage about their names.

閱讀理解 Reading Comprehension

Helpful Vocabulary

可是　　　　　　　kěshì　　　　　　　but

爸爸	bàba	father
所以	suǒyǐ	so; therefore
又	yòu	again
媽媽	māma	mother
花兒	huār	flower
因為	yīnwèi	because; because of; due to
像……一樣	xiàng…yíyàng	as…as

1. Fill in the blanks (one character per blank).

　　王小姐是美國人。她____一個美國名字，也____一個中國____ ____。她的朋友們都____她Mary，可是她父母叫她"美華"。有一天，她問她爸爸，"'美華'是___ ___意思?"她爸爸說，"'美'是美國的___ ___，'華'是中國的意思。你是中國人在美國生的___ ___，所以我們叫你'美華'"。她又問她媽媽，"'美華'是甚麼___ ___?" 媽媽說，"'美'____beautiful的意思，'華'____'花兒'的意思。我們叫你'美華'，因為我們___ ___你像花兒一樣美。"

2. Answer the following questions about the passage.

1) 王小姐為甚麼 (wèishénme, why)有一個美國名字，也有一個中國名字?

2) 她的美國名字叫甚麼? 中國名字呢?

3) 她爸爸說她的中文名字是甚麼意思? 她媽媽呢?

4) 為甚麼爸爸媽媽的回答(huídá, answer)不一樣?

WORDS AND EXPRESSIONS ON SPECIFIC TOPICS
課堂用語 (Expressions Used in Class)

1.	老師	lǎoshī	teacher	18. 學第x課	xué dì...kè	study lesson x
2.	同學	tóngxué	classmate	19. 打開書	dǎkāi shū	open the book
3.	頁	yè	page	20. 合上書	héshàng shū	close the book
4.	行	háng	line	21. 上課	shàngkè	go to class
5.	錄音	lùyīn	recording	22. 下課	xiàkè	finish class
6.	會話	huìhuà	dialogue	23. 念	niàn	read (aloud)
7.	聽寫	tīngxiě	dictation	24. 跟我念	gēn wǒ niàn	read after me
8.	練習	liànxí	exercises	25. 再說一次	zàishuō yícì	say (it) again
9.	回答	huídá	answer	26. 大聲說	dàshēng shuō	say (it) louder
10.	問題	wèntí	question	27. 閱讀	yuèdú	reading
11.	句子	jùzi	sentence	28. 作文	zuòwén	composition
12.	詞	cí	word	29. 黑板	hēibǎn	blackboard
13.	字	zì	character	30. 作業	zuòyè	homework
14.	交	jiāo	submit	31. 填空	tiánkòng	fill in the blanks
15.	發	fā	distribute	32. 對	duì	right
16.	改	gǎi	correct	33. 錯	cuò	wrong
17.	寫字	xiězì	write (characters)			

第二課. 中國人的家庭
Lesson 2. Chinese Families

Before You Read

Getting Started: Study the picture and discuss it.

這家有幾口人？請你介紹一下這家人。

生詞
VOCABULARY

1.	家庭	jiātíng	N	family
2.	大	dà	SV	big
3.	幾	jǐ	Nu./QW	several/how many
4.	代	dài	M	generation
5.	住	zhù	V	to live
6.	在	zài	CV	at; on; in
7.	一起	yìqǐ	Adv.	together
8.	老	lǎo	SV	old
9.	少	shào	SV	young
10.	口	kǒu	N/M	mouth; head (people of a family)
11.	少	shǎo	SV	few
12.	家長	jiāzhǎng	N	the head of a family; patriarch
13.	聽話	tīnghuà	VO/SV	to heed what an elder or superior says; to be obedient
14.	裏	lǐ	Loc.	in; inside
15.	照顧	zhàogù	V	to look after
16.	了	le	Pt.	(indicates a change of state)
17.	以後	yǐhòu	TW	after; later
18.	兄弟	xiōngdì	N	brothers
19.	互相	hùxiāng	Adv.	mutually, each other
20.	幫助	bāngzhù	V	to help
21.	一些	yìxiē	Pron.	some
22.	問題	wèntí	N	problem; question
23.	常常	chángcháng	Adv.	often
24.	替	tì	CV/V	for (take the place of); to replace

25.	自己	zìjǐ	Pron.	self
26.	決定	juédìng	V/N	to decide; decision
27.	應該	yīnggāi	MV	should; ought to
28.	跟	gēn	CV/V	with; and; follow
29.	誰	shéi/shuí	QW	who; whom
30.	結婚	jiéhūn	VO	to marry
31.	還	hái	Adv.	still, yet
32.	只	zhǐ	Adv.	only
33.	想	xiǎng	V/MV	to think; to miss; to want
34.	要	yào	V/MV	to want; to need; to be about to
35.	現在	xiànzài	TW	now; at present
36.	已經	yǐjīng	Adv.	already
37.	現代	xiàndài	N/SV	modern times; modern
38.	和	hé	Conj.	and
39.	啊	a	Pt.	(indicates doubt or questioning)
40.	為甚麼	wèishénme	QW	why
41.	能	néng	MV	to be able to
42.	兩	liǎng	Nu	two (used before a measure word)
43.	這兒	zhèr	PW	here
44.	做	zuò	V	to do
45.	忙	máng	SV	busy
46.	着急	zháojí	SV/V	worried; to feel anxious; to worry
47.	為	wèi	CV	for
48.	事	shì	N	thing; matter
49.	件	jiàn	M	measure word for clothes or matters
50.	說	shuō	V	to speak

51. 主意	zhǔyi	N	idea
52. 明天	míngtiān	TW	tomorrow
53. 生日	shēngrì	N	birthday
54. 給	gěi	CV/V	for (for the benefit of); to; to give
55. 買	mǎi	V	to buy
56. 樣	yàng	N	pattern
57. 東西	dōngxi	N	thing; object
58. 錢	qián	N	money
59. 沒有	méiyǒu	V	do not have; without
60. 對	duì	SV	right
61. 用	yòng	V/CV	to use; with; by means of
62. 這些	zhèxiē	Pron.	these
63. 一共	yígòng	Adv.	altogether
64. 塊	kuài	M	unit of currency; piece
65. 朋友	péngyou	N	friend
66. 介紹	jièshào	V/N	to introduce; introduction
67. 英文	yīngwén	N	English
68. 可以	kěyǐ	MV	may; can
69. 學	xué	V	to study; to learn
70. 嘛	ma	Pt.	(used to emphasize the obvious)

Special Vocabulary

Family Members

爺爺	yéye	N	paternal grandfather
奶奶	nǎinai	N	paternal grandmother
爸爸	bàba	N	father

媽媽	māma	N	mother
哥哥	gēge	N	older brother
姐姐	jiějie	N	older sister
弟弟	dìdi	N	younger brother
妹妹	mèimei	N	younger sister

Numbers

一	yī	Nu.	one
二	èr	Nu.	two
三	sān	Nu.	three
四	sì	Nu.	four
五	wǔ	Nu.	five
六	liù	Nu.	six
七	qī	Nu.	seven
八	bā	Nu.	eight
九	jiǔ	Nu.	nine
十	shí	Nu.	ten
百	bǎi	Nu.	hundred
千	qiān	Nu.	thousand
萬	wàn	Nu.	ten thousand
億	yì	Nu.	hundred million
零	líng	Nu.	zero

First Reading: Getting the Main Ideas

There are four main ideas discussed in the text. These ideas are listed below. Read the text and then number these ideas according to the order in which they appear in the text.

_____ 大家庭的問題。
_____ 以前的中國大家庭是甚麼樣的。
_____ 現代 (xiàndài, modern) 的中國家庭是甚麼樣的。
_____ 在大家庭裏，家裏人的關係(guānxi, relationship)。

中國人的家庭

以前，很多中國人的家庭是大家庭。一家幾代人：爺爺、奶奶、爸爸、媽媽、哥哥、姐姐、弟弟、妹妹都住在一起。男男女女，老老少少，多的幾十口人，少的也有十幾口人。一家有一個家長，一家人都聽家長的話。

在大家庭裏，父母照顧孩子。父母老了以後，孩子也要照顧父母。兄弟姐妹也都互相幫助。

中國的大家庭也有一些問題。比方說，父母常常替自己的孩子決定他們應該跟誰結婚；還有很多家庭只想要男孩子，不想要女孩子。

現在，在中國，大家庭已經不多了。現代的中國家庭常常只有三口人 — 父母跟一個孩子。

Second Reading: Getting the Specific Information

Reread the text and indicate whether the following statements are true or false. Write "T" for true and "F" for false. If the statement is false, correct it.

____ 1. 中國以前的大家庭常常是幾代人住在一起。

____ 2. 在大家庭裏，家長說話沒有人聽。

____ 3. 父母老了以後，孩子應該照顧父母。

____ 4. 哥哥應該幫助弟弟、妹妹；弟弟、妹妹不應該幫助哥哥。

____ 5. 在以前的大家庭裏，父母都不希望生兒子 (érzi, son)。

____ 6. 很多中國現代的家庭都只有一個孩子。

Understanding the Text Structure

There are four main ideas in the text. Each main idea is supported by specific details. Match each specific detail to the main idea it supports.

Main Ideas	Details
1. 中國的大家庭是甚麼樣的	___ 一個家庭有三口人
2. 在大家庭裏，家裏人的關係	___ 父母常常決定孩子跟誰結婚
3. 大家庭的問題	___ 一家人都要聽家長的話
4. 現代的中國家庭	___ 很多家庭都希望多生兒子
	___ 幾代人住在一起
	___ 父母老了，孩子要照顧父母
	___ 兄弟姐妹都應該互相幫助

會話
DIALOGUES

(一)

(Miss Zhang is an American-born Chinese touring Mainland China. She is eager to learn Chinese culture. The following is a conversation between her and a child named Xiaoduo Wang.)

張：小朋友，你叫甚麼名字？

王：我叫小多。

張：你家有幾口人？

王：我家有三口人：爸爸、媽媽、和我。

張：你沒有兄弟姐妹嗎？

王：沒有。

張：你想要嗎？

王：想啊！我想要個弟弟。我問爸爸，我為甚麼不能有個弟弟？他說一家只能有一個孩子。可是他自己有一個哥哥、兩個姐姐、三個弟弟、四個妹妹！

Practice: Work in pairs

Each partner asks the other in turn how many family members each one has, who they are, and what they do.

（二）

(Old Zhang and Old Wang have been friends for many years. One day Old Zhang finds Old Wang walking back and forth and looking worried. He is concerned.)

張：老王，你在這兒忙甚麼呢？

王：我在這兒着急呢。

張：你為甚麼事着急啊？

王：有很多事呢！

張：你跟我説説，我替你想個主意。

王：一件事是：明天是我太太的生日，我想給她買個東西。

張：你想給她買一個甚麼樣的東西呢？

王：這個東西要很多錢。

張：你沒有錢，對不對？你用我的錢買吧。一百、兩百，這一共是兩百三十二塊，都給你。

王：謝謝你！

張：還有甚麼事？

王：我大兒子還沒有女朋友。

張：我可以給他介紹一個。

王：我小兒子的英文不好。

張：他可以跟我學嘛。

Practice: Work in pairs

Your friend gets terribly sick. Tell the class what you can do to help. Include the words 在，為，跟，替，給，and 用 in your statement.

語法介紹
GRAMMATICAL POINTS

Numbers

There are fifteen basic numerals in general use:
一，二，三，四，五，六，七，八，九，十，百，千，萬，億，零。All Chinese numbers are formed by one of the fifteen basic numerals or a combination of them. For example:

1	一	25	二十五
10	十	300	三百
12	十二	4,321	四千三百二十一
20	二十	80,100	八萬零一百

幾 refers to an approximate number meaning several (no more than ten).

1. 他有幾個孩子。

    He has several children (meaning between three and nine).

2. 她家有十幾口人。

    In her family there are more than ten people (but fewer than twenty).

3. 他家有幾十口人。

    In his family there are several tens of people (but fewer than one hundred).

Use 二 when you count, but use 兩 when followed by a measure word. For example, 他有兩個孩子。

Measure Words

Measure words are words that are used to indicate units. There are many measure words in Chinese. Different nouns require different measure words. For example, the measure word for counting 家庭 is 個, but the measure word for counting family members is 口. When a number is not indicated, the use of a measure word may not be necessary. For example, 他有孩子。However, when a number is used, a measure word normally must be included. For example, 他有兩個孩子。*他有兩孩子 is not acceptable. When the number is one, the number can be omitted. For example, 他有個孩子。

Noun Phrases

A number, a measure word, and other elements can form a noun phrase. A noun phrase may appear in the following forms:

Form 1: Num + M + N

他有兩個孩子。

Form 2: Num + M + Modifier + N

他有兩個男孩子。

Form 3: Pro. + Num + M + (Modifier) N

這幾個孩子不姓張，那兩個女孩子姓張。

Coverbs

Coverbs are verbs such as 在，為，跟，用, etc., which introduce phrases that denote the place, time, interest, purpose, reason, means, or manner in which an action takes place. Coverbs serve the same function as prepositions in English. They are called coverbs, not prepositions, because they carry many characteristics of verbs. For example, modal verbs and adverbs can be placed before them.

Form: Subj. + Coverb + O + V + O

1. 你在這兒做甚麼？   (place 在: at, on, in)
2. 你為甚麼事着急啊？   (purpose 為: for, for the sake of)
3. 你跟我說說。   (association 跟: with, to)
4. 你用我的錢買吧。   (means 用: with, by means of)
5. 你替我說吧。   (manner 替: for; to replace)
6. 他想給我介紹一個女朋友。   (purpose 給: for, for the benefit of)

The following sentences show examples of where modal verbs and adverbs are placed before the coverbs:

1. 他不在這兒學中文。
2. 請別 (bié, don't) 為我的事着急。
3. 他想跟你說說。
4. 你可以用我的錢買。

句型和詞匯用法
SENTENCE PATTERNS AND WORD USAGE

Study the following examples and create a sentence using each phrase or pattern.

一些/這些/那些/哪些 (nǎxie, which)

1. 中國的大家庭也有一些問題。
2. 這些東西我都想買。
3. 那些人都是你的朋友嗎?
4. 你想去哪些地方?
5. _____ 。

以後

1. 父母老了以後,孩子要照顧父母。
2. 以後,你們要聽父母的話。
3. 結婚以後她還跟父母住在一起。
4. 我決定以後不要孩子。
5. _____ 。

想

1. 很多家庭只想要男孩子。
2. 他常常想這個問題。
3. 她很想她父母。
4. 她不想跟他結婚。
5. _____ 。

能

1. 我為甚麼不能有個弟弟?
2. 你不能跟他結婚。
3. 在中國,一家能要幾個孩子?
4. _____ 。

練習
EXERCISES

語音練習 Pronunciation

1. Write the pinyin romanization for the underlined characters.

一起	互相	主意	姐妹	介紹
以前	想要	已經	結婚	不少
跟誰	小孩	東西	問題	照顧
很多	多少	四個	時間	着急

2. Write the characters for the following; pay special attention to the underlined syllables.

yīnggāi	zìjǐ	hénshǎo
yīngguó	míngzi	jièshào
péngyou	yǐqián	zhù zài yīqǐ
yǒuqián	yǒuqián	bāngzhù

漢字練習 Chinese Characters

1. Find the meaning for each of the following radicals in the section "Learning Characters" in the introduction.

子 _____

宀 _____

言 _____

2. Find words with these radicals in the text and write them below.

_____

詞彙練習 **Vocabulary Practice**

1. Use the following characters to form different words.

家：他家有十口人，是一個大____ ____。

　　他爸爸是他家的____ ____。

以：____ ____一家常常有十幾口人。

　　結婚____ ____，他就不跟父母住在一起了。

　　你____ ____給我兒子介紹一個女朋友吧？

些：你還有____ ____問題？我想我可以幫幫你。

　　____ ____東西是你的嗎？

　　明天我要用____ ____錢。

少：你覺得 (juéde, think) 家裏人口多好？還是人口____好？

　　小李家老____ ____ ____一共有九口人。

現：你____ ____可以決定嗎？

　　____ ____的家庭都是小家庭。

2. Fill in each blank with the appropriate word from among the following.

　　　互相　聽話　照顧　已經　一起　決定　着急　幫助

a. 你們_____替我想個主意，好不好？

b. 你的話對我很有_____。

c. 我們都是朋友，應該_____幫助。

d. 你應該做一個_____的孩子。

e. 老王常常替我_____我的兩個孩子。

f. 他_____有女朋友了。

g. 他們兩個人_____明天結婚。

h. 老王常常為兒子的事_____。

語法練習 **Grammar**

1. Match the Chinese expression in Column B with its counterpart in Column A.

Column A	Column B
16____	a. 四百
59____	b. 一億
308____	c. 十六
400____	d. 一萬八千
1,942____	e. 七千二百零五
7,205____	f. 一百萬
18,000____	g. 五十九
108,000____	h. 三百零八
1,000,000____	i. 一千九百四十二
100,000,000____	j. 十萬零八千

2. Write the following numbers in Chinese characters.

Example: 15 十五

22 _____   101 _____   37 _____   18 _____

510 _____   49 _____   476 _____   199 _____

3. Complete the following sentences using the information provided.

1) 老王有 _____ 。(two children)
2) 他家有 _____ 。(ten family members)
3) 一年有 _____ 。(365 days)
4) _____ 是我的。(these three children)
5) 這是 _____ 大家庭。(one)
6) 生孩子是_____ 大事。(a person's)
7) 我喜歡 (xǐhuan, like) _____ 地方。(this)

4. Fill in the blanks with coverbs.

1) 父母常常_____孩子的事着急。

2) 我_____家不常常說中文。

3) 你能_____我介紹個女朋友嗎?

4) 我可以_____我媽媽學中文。

5) 你應該_____自己的錢買。

6) 他想_____小王結婚。

7) 我要_____你買一件好東西。

8) 他有時間嗎? 請你_____我問問他。

9) 甚麼事啊? 你能不能_____我說說?

10) 學中文是你自己的事, 我不能_____你學。

綜合練習 Comprehensive Exercises

1. Read the passage and fill in the blanks.

　　王小小家是一____十幾____人的大家庭。他家有爺爺、奶奶、爸爸、媽媽, ____有他們兄弟姐妹五個。老大是男孩兒, 老二是女的, 小小是老____, 老四是個弟弟, 最小 (zuì xiǎo, the youngest) 的是妹妹。小小的父母在家要____老的, 也要照顧小的。王小小的大哥已經_____了, 他太太在大學教 (jiāo, teach) 中文。他們有兩個孩子: 一個兒子, 一個____ ____。他們一家四口都跟父母住在____ ____。王小小的姐姐也不小了, 可是還沒有_____朋友。小小一家人都很_____這件事著急。一天, 小小跟姐姐說: "姐姐, 我給你介紹一個人, 他是我的朋友。"姐姐說: "甚麼? 你的朋友? 你的朋友都是小男孩兒! 我怎麼能_____小孩兒做朋友呢?" 王小小不說話了, 他想第二天跟大哥說說, 請他給姐姐____ ____一個。

2. Reread the passage and indicate whether the following statements are true or false.

____1) 小小的父母有五個孩子。

____2) 小小是男的。

____3) 小小的父母很忙。

____4) 老大, 老二都結婚了。

____5) 小小的大哥結婚以後不在父母家住了。

____6) 大哥的太太的中文不太好。

____小小想幫他姐姐。

____小小的姐姐不想要弟弟的朋友做男朋友。

口語練習 Oral Exercise

1. Talk about your own family.

2. Discuss the advantages and disadvantages of the traditional Chinese extended family.

寫作練習 Writing

Write a short essay about your family: 我的家。

閱讀練習 Reading Comprehension

Read the passage quickly, without using a dictionary, and answer the questions that follow.

　　我叫王大海，今年十四歲。我有一個弟弟叫王二海，今年十歲，我們都是在上海出生的。我還有兩個妹妹，一個五歲，叫美英；一個三歲，叫美華。她們都是在美國出生的。我們一家都聽我爸爸的話。要是爸爸不在家，他們就聽我的，因為我是男孩子，也是老大。我有爺爺，也有奶奶，可是他們不跟我們一起住。我爺爺只喜歡男孩子，不喜歡女孩子，所以他很喜歡我和我弟弟，不太喜歡我的兩個妹妹。

問題：

1. 我家一共有幾口人？

2. 我們兄弟姐妹一共有幾個人？

3. 誰是我家的家長？

4. 我爺爺為甚麼不喜歡我的妹妹？

5. 為甚麼我和弟弟的名字都有 "海" 這個字？

WORDS AND EXPRESSIONS ON SPECIFIC TOPICS
錢 (Money)

1.	美元	měiyuán	U.S. dollar
2.	日元	rìyuán	Japanese yen
3.	英鎊	yīngbàng	pound sterling
4.	元	yuán	Chinese monetary unit (formal)
5.	一百元	yìbǎi yuán	100 yuan
6.	塊	kuài	Chinese monetary unit (informal)
7.	兩塊五	liǎng kuài wǔ	2.50 yuan
8.	角	jiǎo	10 cents (formal)
9.	兩角(錢)	liǎn jiǎo (qián)	0.20 yuan
10.	毛	máo	10 cents (informal)
11.	五毛(錢)	wǔ máo (qián)	0.50 yuan
12.	分	fēn	cent
13.	三分(錢)	sān fēn (qián)	0.03 yuan
14.	二十塊零五分	èrshí kuài líng wǔ fēn	20.05 yuan
15.	九毛九	jiǔ máo jiǔ	0.99 yuan
16.	一共多少錢?	yígòng duōshǎo qián	How much altogether?
17.	幾塊/毛/分錢	jǐ kuài/máo/fēn	How much?
18.	十塊多	shí kuài duō	more than 10 yuan and less than 11 yuan
19.	幾十塊	jǐshí kuài	several tens
20.	不到十塊	búdào shí kuài	less than ten yuan

第三課. 大江南北

Lesson 3. China

Before You Read

Getting Started: Study the map and discuss the following.

1. 長江在中國的甚麼地方?
2. 中國的南方和北方有甚麼不一樣?

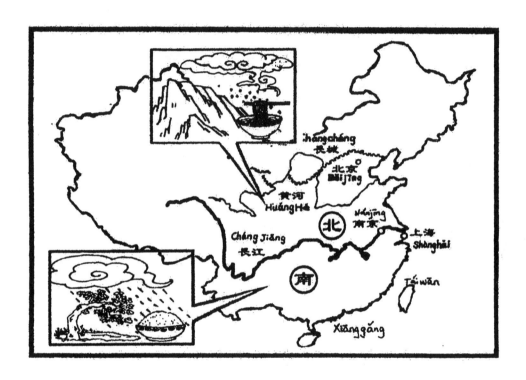

生詞
VOCABULARY

1.	高	gāo	SV	high, tall
2.	山	shān	N	mountain
3.	河	hé	N	river
4.	最	zuì	Adv.	most (used to form superlative)
5.	條	tiáo	M	measure word for river and various long, narrow things
6.	部	bù	Loc.	part, section
7.	長江	Chángjiāng	PN	Yangtze River
8.	南	nán	N	south
9.	邊	biān	N/Loc.	side
10.	南方	nánfāng	N	the south
11.	夏天	xiàtiān	N	summer
12.	熱	rè	SV	hot
13.	下雨	xiàyǔ	VO	to rain
14.	那裏	nàlǐ	PW	there
15.	湖	hú	N	lake
16.	樹	shù	N	tree
17.	愛	ài	MV/V	to love
18.	吃	chī	V	to eat
19.	魚	yú	N	fish
20.	大米	dàmǐ	N	rice (uncooked rice)
21.	北	běi	N	north
22.	北方	běifāng	N	the north
23.	一樣	yíyàng	SV	same

24.	冬天	dōngtiān	N	winter
25.	冷	lěng	SV	cold
26.	下雪	xiàxuě	VO	to snow
27.	那兒	nàr	PW	there
28.	因為……所以	yīnwèi…suǒyǐ	Conj.	because . . . so . . .
29.	麵	miàn	N	(wheat) flour
30.	西	xī	N	west
31.	東	dōng	N	east
32.	低	dī	SV/V	low; to lower
33.	從	cóng	Prep.	from
34.	往	wǎng	Prep.	toward
35.	流	liú	V	to flow
36.	寬	kuān	SV	wide
37.	窄	zhǎi	SV	narrow
38.	兩邊	liǎngbiān	PW	both sides
39.	好看	hǎokàn	SV	pretty; good-looking
40.	城市	chéngshì	N	city
41.	經過	jīngguò	V	to pass through
42.	首都	shǒudū	N	capital
43.	前頭	qiántou	PW	in front
44.	房子	fángzi	N	house
45.	面	miàn	N/Loc.	side
46.	左	zuǒ	N/Loc.	left
47.	右	yòu	N/Loc.	right
48.	中間	zhōngjiān	PW	middle

49. 真	zhēn	Adv.	really; truly
50. 後頭	hòutou	PW	behind
51. 所	suǒ	M	measure word for buildings
52. 外	wài	Loc.	outside
53. 旁邊	pángbiān	PW	side
54. 棵	kē	M	measure word for tree, etc.
55. 下	xià	Loc.	under
56. 累	lèi	SV	tired
57. 哪兒	nǎr	QW	where
58. 樓	lóu	N	storied building; floor
59. 工作	gōngzuò	V/N	to work; job
60. 書	shū	N	book

First Reading: Getting the Main Ideas

There are three main ideas in the text. After reading the text, circle the phrases below that express the main ideas.

1. 中國的高山和大河。
2. 長江在中國的甚麼地方。
3. 南方人和北方人不一樣。
4. 南方人愛吃甚麼，北方人愛吃甚麼。
5. 中國的南方和北方。
6. 長江經過的地方。

大江南北

中國地方很大，有很多高山跟大河，最長的一條河在中國的中部，叫長江。

長江的南邊是中國的南方。南方夏天很熱，常常下雨，那裏山多，湖多，樹也多。南方人愛吃魚和大米。長江的北邊是中國的北方。中國的北方跟南方很不一樣。北方冬天很冷，常常下雪。北方高山也不少，可是湖少，樹也少。北方人愛吃麵，不常吃米。

因為中國西邊高，東邊低，所以很多大河都從西往東流，長江也是一樣。長江有的地方寬，有的地方窄，有的地方江的兩邊都是山，很好看；有的地方兩邊都是城市。長江經過的最後一個城市是上海。上海是中國最大的城市。中國的首都是北京。北京在長江的北邊，是一個北方城市。

Second Reading: Getting the Specific Information

Reread the text and circle the correct choice for each statement based on the text.

1. 長江在中國的____。　　　　a.西部　　　b.中部　　　c.南部
2. 北方____少。　　　　　　　a.高山　　　b.湖　　　　c.雪
3. 南方夏天____下雨。　　　　a.不愛　　　b.不常　　　c.常常
4. 北方人出生在長江的____。　a.東邊　　　b.南邊　　　c.北邊
5. 南方人不常吃____。　　　　a.米　　　　b.麵　　　　c.魚
6. 北方人不常吃____。　　　　a.米　　　　b.麵　　　　c.魚
7. 中國東邊____。　　　　　　a.高　　　　b.低　　　　c.寬
8. 長江從____往____流。　　　a.東/西　　 b.南/北　　 c.西/東
9. 長江經過很多的____。　　　a.樹　　　　b.湖　　　　c.城市
10. ____是長江經過的最後一個城市。　　　a.北京　　　b.上海

Understanding the Text Structure

1. The passage in this lesson uses the Yangtze River as a line of demarcation to describe the geography of China. The predominant structure of the passage uses contrasting expressions to show contrasting features.
The words signaling contrast in this lesson include: 多 vs. 少, 常常 vs. 不常, 有 vs. 沒有, etc. Fill in the blanks below with expressions that contrast with the words given.

冷_____　　高_____　　寬_____　　南_____　　大_____

一樣_____　好看_____　南方_____　東邊_____　冬天_____

2. In the second paragraph, southern China and northern China are contrasted in three ways. Find all the points of relevant information from the text and write them in the appropriate places.

	南方	北方
a. Climate	_____	_____
b. Geographical information	_____	_____
c. Eating habits	_____	_____

會話
Dialogue

(Xiao Wang is showing a family photo to his colleague Xiao Gao.)

小高：樹前頭的這三個人是誰啊？

小王：左邊的是我，右邊的是我太太，中間的那個是我女兒。

小高：你們後頭的那所房子是不是你家？

小王：是啊。

小高：你家這兒真美啊！房子前頭有樹，後頭有山。

小王：是啊。這是城外嘛！你看，我家旁邊還有一個小湖。我常常在湖邊的那棵大樹下看書。累了，就看看湖裏的魚。你家在哪兒啊？

小高：我家在城裏。那兒都是高樓，人太多，沒有湖，樹也很少。

Practice: Work in pairs

Each partner tells the other something about his or her hometown and the surrounding area.

語法介紹
GRAMMATICAL POINTS

Place Words

Place words refer to a locality. There are basically five types of place words. The following lists the types and rules for using place words.

Type 1. Proper Name of Specific Place

中國, 美國, 上海

Type 2. Direction + Suffix

(Among this category, there are a few place words that are not direction and suffix combinations, such as 中間, 底下, and 旁邊. Moreover, there are no 左頭 and 右頭 in Chinese.)

Form:	Direction	suffix
	上	頭
	下	邊
	前	面
	後	部
	左	
	右	
	裏	
	外	
	東	
	南	
	西	
	北	

Type 3. Place Words That Tell About the General Position of the Person or Thing in Reference to the Speaker

這兒/這裏/這邊/這面

那兒/那裏/那邊/那面

哪兒/哪裏/哪邊/哪面

Type 4. Place Words That Tell About the Exact Locality of an Entity Relative to a Specific Thing.

Form:	Noun + direction (+ suffix)			
	樹	上	(頭/邊/面)	on the top of the tree
	湖	裏	(頭/邊/面)	in the lake
	樓	前	(頭/邊/面)	in front of the building

Type 5. Place Words That Refer to the Position of Something That Is Near or Far from the Speaker

Form:　　N +　　這兒/這裏/這邊/這面

　　　　　　　　那兒/那裏/那邊/那面

　　　　　　　　哪兒/哪裏/哪邊/哪面

e.g., 我這兒/小王那裏/山哪邊

Use of Place Words

In describing places, 有 and 在 are frequently used.

Form:　　PW + 有 + N

1. 中國有很多高山。
2. 前邊有人嗎?
3. 哪兒有河?
4. 湖裏有沒有魚?
5. 樓那兒沒有樹。

Form:　　N + 在 + PW

6. 他家在上海。
7. 小王在裏面嗎?

8. 你家在哪兒?
9. 老李在不在樓上?
10. 錢不在我這兒。

句型和詞匯用法
SENTENCE PATTERNS AND WORD USAGE

Study the following examples and create a sentence using each phrase or pattern.

最

1. 中國最大的一條河在中國的中部。
2. 這是我最喜歡的地方。
3. 英國哪個城市最美?
4. _____。

一樣

1. 中國的北方跟南方很不一樣。
2. 他的名字跟你的一樣。
3. 一樣的東西為甚麼錢不一樣?
4. _____。

(因為)……所以……

1. 因為中國西邊高東邊低,所以很多大河都從西往東流。
2. 因為父母的話常常是對的,所以你應該聽父母的話。
3. 他沒有女朋友,所以想請我給他介紹一個。
4. 他想要一個男孩兒,因為他媽媽想要一個孫子(sūnzi, grandson)。
5. _____。

練習
EXERCISES

語音練習 Pronunciation

1. Write the pinyin romanization for the underlined characters.

往東流	互相	因為	時間
住在一起	大湖	英文	一件
小孩	城市	很窄	都是
大海	從西往東	在家	首都

2. Write the characters for the following; pay special attention to the underlined syllable.

dìfang	xuéyīngwén	chángjiāng
dìdi	xiàxuě	chángyòng
xiàtiān	nǎr	dōngtiān
xiàyǔ	nàr	dōngfāng

漢字練習 Chinese Characters

1. Write the meaning of the following radicals.

氵 _____

土 _____

冫 _____

雨 _____

Lesson 3. China   51

2. Using the meaning of the radicals, guess the meaning of the following words. Match the translation to the characters. (Do not use a dictionary.)

池 _____   a. freeze

漁人 _____ b. thunder

坑 _____   c. pit

坡地 _____ d. pond

冰河 _____ e. white cloud

雷 _____   f. fisherman

白雲 _____ g. sloping fields

凍 _____   h. glacier

詞匯練習 Vocabulary Practice

1. Write the antonym of each of the following.

高____   大____   寬____   冷____

上____   左____   前____   裏____

2. Write the character indicated by the pinyin.

xià ____邊 ____天   míng ____字 ____天

bù   ____好 西____   shì   不____ 城____

hé   大____ 你____他   jīng 已____ 北____

3. Fill in the blank with the correct measure word.

一____河   兩____江   三____湖   四____魚

五____樹   六____房子 七____城市 八____地方

語法練習 **Grammar**

1. Circle the correct choice for each sentence.

    1) 南方____很多湖。　　　　　　　　有　　　在

    2) 上海____長江的最東邊。　　　　有　　　在

    3) 你家____哪兒?　　　　　　　　　　有　　　在

    4) 樹下____有人。　　　　　　　　　　不　　　沒

    5) 北京____在南方。　　　　　　　　　不　　　沒

    6) 你們____的那個人是你妹妹嗎?　裏邊　　中間

    7) 你的東西在我_____。　　　　　　這兒　　那兒

    8) 我的書在他_____。　　　　　　　　這兒　　那兒

2. Using the map in the "Before You Read" section, answer the following questions.

    1) 中國有哪幾條大河?

    2) 北京在哪兒?

    3) 南京在哪兒?

    4) 上海在哪兒?

    5) 中國北方最大的城市是甚麼地方?

    6) 中國南方最大的城市是甚麼地方?

    7) 臺灣 (Taiwan) 在哪兒?

    8) 香港 (Hong Kong) 在哪兒?

綜合練習 **Comprehensive Exercises**

Helpful Vocabulary

平原	píngyuán	plain
人口	rénkǒu	population
古	gǔ	ancient

中心	zhōngxīn	center
天安門	Tiān'ānmén	Tiananmen

Read the following passage and fill in the blanks.

  北京_____中國的東部。北京的北邊和西_____都是山，東邊是大海，東南邊是平原。北京是一個北方_____，那兒_____很冷，常常下大雪；夏天很_____，常常下大雨，下雨_____就不那麼熱了。北京的春天和秋天都很好，應該說秋天最好，不_____也不熱。

  北京是一個古城，在八百多年_____就已經是都城了。都城就是我們現在說的首都。北京有很多有名的地方。比方說，市中心有大家都知道的天安門，城外的山上_____長城。

  現在的_____也是一個現代大城市，有一千萬人口 (rénkǒu, population)。城裏_____有很多高樓。

口語練習 Oral Exercise

Compare one aspect of China and America. How are they similar and how are they different?

寫作練習 Writing

Write a letter to a friend or a member of your family about your impression or your experience of a place you have visited. Model your letter on the next exercise.

閱讀練習 Reading Comprehension

1. Read the following letter quickly, without using a dictionary. When you see a word you do not know, guess the meaning from the context.
2. Answer the questions after reading.

小妹：

  你好嗎？爸媽好嗎？我來上海已經十幾天了。我現在很忙，也很累，因為我每天都有很多工作。

我不喜歡上海。這兒人太多，住的地方太小，樹也太少。這幾天這兒很熱。

　　我真想家。咱家那兒多好啊！房子大，前邊後邊都是樹。樹林裏有那麼多小動物。還有房子後邊的那個小湖，裏頭的小魚多好看啊！我以前常常在樹下頭看書，在湖邊看魚。我真希望我現在不在上海。這樣我們兩人就可以一起在湖邊看魚了。

　　我不在家，你要聽爸媽的話，多照顧弟弟。替我問爸媽好！

　　祝好！

姐姐：美真
八月二十日

問題：

1. 美真現在在哪兒工作？

2. 美真為甚麼不喜歡上海？

3. 美真家跟上海有甚麼不一樣的地方？

WORDS AND EXPRESSIONS ON SPECIFIC TOPICS
方位 (Locations)

1. 左邊	zuǒbiān	left side	12. 桌子 (zhuōzi) 右面		on the right side of the table
2. 下面	xiàmian	lower level	13. 椅子 (yǐzi) 前頭		in front of the chair
3. 外頭	wàitou	outside	14. 電腦 (diànnǎo) 那兒		over there where the computer is
4. 東部	dōngbù	east	15. 書架 (shūjià) 旁邊		beside the book shelf
5. 中間	zhōngjiān	between; center	16. 書包 (shūbāo) 裏		in the schoolbag
6. 底下	dǐxia	under; below	17. 床 (chuáng) 底下		under the bed
7. 旁邊	pángbiān	beside	18. 牆 (qiáng) 上		on the wall
8. 這兒	zhèr	here	19. 窗戶 (chuānghu) 外邊		outside the window
9. 那邊	nàbiān	there	20. 教室 (jiàoshì) 的中間		in the middle of the classroom
10. 哪裏	nǎlǐ	where	21. 我的筆 (bǐ) 在哪兒?		Where is my pen?
11. 右面	yòumiàn	to the right	22. 門 (mén) 前有一棵樹。		There is a tree in front of the door.

第四課. 十個太陽

Lesson 4. The Ten Suns

Before You Read

Getting Started: Study the picture and discuss it.

要是 (yàoshi, if) 天上有十個太陽，地上會有甚麼問題？

生詞
VOCABULARY

1.	古	gǔ	SV	ancient
2.	時候	shíhou	TW/N	time; when . . .
3.	天	tiān	N	sky; heaven
4.	太陽	tàiyáng	N	sun
5.	長得	zhǎngde	V	to grow up to look like . . .
6.	完全	wánquán	Adv.	completely; entirely; absolutely
7.	每	měi	Adj.	every
8.	到	dào	V/CV	to arrive; to reach; to
9.	去	qù	V	to go
10.	東方	dōngfāng	N	the east
11.	最後	zuìhòu	Adv./SV	finally; the last
12.	飛	fēi	V	to fly
13.	西方	xīfāng	N	the west
14.	回	huí	V	to return; to go back
15.	就是	jiùshì	V	namely; to be no other than
16.	知道	zhīdào	V	to know; to realize; to be aware of
17.	覺得	juéde	V	to sense; to feel
18.	有意思	yǒuyìsi	SV	interesting
19.	第	dì	Prefix	ordinal number prefix
20.	一塊兒	yíkuàir	Adv.	together
21.	如果	rúguǒ	Conj.	if; in case
22.	看見	kànjiàn	VP	to see
23.	那麼	nàme	Conj.	then; therefore

24.	會	huì	MV/V	will; would; to know how to . . .
25.	非常	fēicháng	Adv.	extremely; unusually; extraordinarily
26.	地上	dìshang	N	(on) the ground; on the earth
27.	馬上	mǎshàng	Adv.	immediately
28.	變得	biànde	VP	to become
29.	死	sǐ	V	to die
30.	神	shén	N	god; spiritual being
31.	事情	shìqing	N	matter; event; thing; business
32.	生氣	shēngqì	V/SV	to get angry; to take offense; angry
33.	叫	jiào	V	to ask; to order; to call; to shout
34.	力氣	lìqi	N	physical strength; effort
35.	射	shè	V	to shoot
36.	箭	jiàn	N	arrow
37.	羿	Yì	PN	the name of the god who, according to legend, shot down nine suns
38.	難過	nánguò	SV	sad; aggrieved
39.	跑	pǎo	V	run
40.	過日子	guò rìzi	VO	to live (one's life)
41.	昨天	zuótiān	TW	yesterday
42.	晚上	wǎnshang	N	evening
43.	天氣	tiānqì	N	weather
44.	吃飯	chīfàn	VO	to eat (a meal); to have a meal
45.	怕	pà	V	to be afraid; fear
46.	總算	zǒngsuàn	Adv.	finally; at last
47.	舒服	shūfu	SV	comfortable
48.	睡	shuì	V	to sleep

49. 季節	jìjié	N	season (of the year)
50. 風	fēng	N	wind

First Reading: Getting the Main Ideas

Read the following story quickly and answer the questions based on the text:

古時候天上有幾個太陽？為甚麼現在只有一個太陽了？

十個太陽

古時候，天上有十個太陽。這十個太陽長得完全一樣，他們都住在東方一棵很高的樹上。

每天，這十個太陽中的一個從樹上飛到天上去。他從東方飛到西方，最後飛回樹上，這就是一天。因為這十個太陽長得一樣，所以人們不知道天上一共有十個太陽。

有一天，這些太陽覺得每天只有一個飛到天上去太沒有意思了，就決定第二天一塊兒飛到天上去。他們想，如果人們看見天上有那麼多太陽，一定會很高興。

第二天這些太陽都飛到天上以後，地上變得非常熱，很多人、樹和動物都熱死了。天神馬上就知道了這件事，他非常生氣，就叫最會射箭的羿到地上來幫助人們。

羿來到地上，看見死了那麼多人，非常難過。他馬上跑到最高的山上去，用箭射那些太陽。第一個太陽射下來以後，他又射第二個。羿一共射下了九個太陽。天上只有一個太陽了，人們又過上了好日子。

Second Reading: Getting the Specific Information

Reread the story and indicate whether the following statements are true or false. Write "T" for true and "F" for false.

____ 1. 十個太陽都住在天上。

____ 2. 人們知道天上有十個太陽，可是他們覺得沒關係，因為這十個太陽每天只有一個飛到天上去。

____ 3. 有一天十個太陽一塊兒飛到天上去了，因為他們覺得這樣有意思。

____ 4. 十個太陽都在天上的時候，地上非常熱，很多人都死了。

____ 5. 天神看見很多人和樹都死了，非常生氣，就到地上來幫助人們。

____ 6. 羿為了幫助人們，射下了十個太陽。

Understanding the Text Structure

This lesson is a narrative text in which a series of events in time are depicted and related through a causal chain.

1. List all the time words in this lesson.

   _____

2. Put these events in the story in order by number.

   _____ 羿到高山上去。

   _____ 十個太陽都一塊兒到天上去。

   _____ 羿用箭射太陽。

   _____ 天神叫羿到地上來。

   _____ 十個太陽每天有一個從東方飛到西方。

   _____ 天上只有一個太陽了。

   _____ 地上變得很熱。

3. Explain the reasons for the following situations.

   古代天上有十個太陽，可是人們不知道，因為_____

   地上死了非常多的人，因為_____

   十個太陽決定一塊兒到天上去，因為_____

   天上的神很生氣，因為_____

   神叫羿到地上來，因為_____

   羿到地上以後很難過，因為_____

Lesson 4. The Ten Suns   63

會話
DIALOGUES

（一）

(It is a fine Sunday morning. 方江 and 張明 leave the city to enjoy the countryside.)

方：這個地方真美！有山，有湖，還有這麼多好看的樹和花。

張：是啊！昨天晚上還下大雨，可是現在你看，太陽就要出來了！

方：天氣這麼好，我們到山上去看看吧。

張：好啊。可是我想吃了飯再去。你說山上會不會太熱？

方：我想不會那麼熱吧。如果真的很熱，我也不怕，我喜歡太陽。我最不喜歡的就是下雨天。謝天謝地！下了幾天的雨，今天總算不下了！

張：那前幾天下大雨，你一定很不舒服了？

方：是啊，我那幾個晚上都沒睡好。

（二）

(Two friends discuss the weather in 上海.)

張：你最喜歡上海的甚麼季節？

王：我最喜歡秋天，因為那兒的秋天很舒服，不冷也不熱。

張：我喜歡上海的春天，因為春天花很多。

王：那你喜歡上海的夏天嗎？

張：上海的夏天不好，太熱了，還常常下大雨。

王：冬天呢？

張：上海的冬天也不好。冬天太冷，風也很大，有時候還下雪。

> **Practice:** Find a partner to talk about the weather in your hometown.

語法介紹
GRAMMATICAL POINTS

The Functions of 了

了 occurs in two prominent positions. One position is at the end of a sentence, which is called "sentence-final 了" (abbreviated here as "sentence 了"). The other occurs after a verb, which is commonly called "verb-suffix 了."

Sentence-Final 了 (Sentence- 了)

The general functions with sentence- 了 introduced in this lesson indicate

1. change of state

    a. 天上只有一個太陽了。

    b. 冬天來了，天氣冷了。

    c. 下了幾天的雨，今天總算不下了。

2. the condition of being excessive (together with 太)

    a. 這些太陽覺得每天只有一個飛到天上去太沒有意思了。

    b. 上海的夏天太熱了!

3. imminent future action—used with 就(要), 要, or 快(要)

(Both 就 and 快 are adverbs, used to indicate that something will happen soon.)

   a. 太陽就要出來了!

   b. A：上海快到了嗎? B：快了!

4. accomplished event

   a. 第二天，這些太陽就一起飛到天上去了。

   b. A：昨天你看中文書了嗎? B：看了。(Neg. 沒看。)

Verb Suffix 了 (Verb- 了)

The verb with suffix 了 denoting *completion of an action or activity*. The verb has to be an "action verb" that is capable of definite termination. Typical situations where verb-suffix 了 is used are:

1. with quantified/specified objects

   Pattern: S (Adv.) V-了 *quantified/specified* (de) Object (or complement)

   a. 這十個太陽在天上飛了很多年。
   b. 羿一共射下了九個太陽。
   c. 下了幾天的雨,今天總算不下了。
   d. 人們又過上了好日子。

2. as the first action that *must be completed* before the next action

   Pattern: S V1-了 (就/才) V2   (See grammar notes for 就 and 才 in this lesson.)

   a. 你得 (děi, must) 看了書才能出去。
   b. 太陽出來了天氣就好了。

3. with verbs that have a built-in terminal point: e.g., 死 (sǐ, to die)了, 忘 (wàng, to forget)了, 掉 (diào, to drop)了, 破 (pò, to break)了.

   a. 很多人、樹、和動物都死了。
   b. 我忘了這個字是甚麼意思。

Note that in 3a the verb suffix 了 happens to be at the end of the sentence. In this case, 了 would indicate both "change of state" and "completion of the action."

Combination of Verb-了 and Sentence-了

When verb-了 and sentence-了 are combined, it indicates the past action has progressed to the present or has current relevance. It is often used with 已經.

   Pattern: S (已經) V-了 *quantity* 的 O 了

   a. 我們已經學了一年的中文了。
   b. 已經下了三天雨了。

Time Elapsed Without Doing Something

Compare the two patterns below:

Pattern 1: S *how long* 沒-V (past time frame)

   a. 我那幾個晚上都沒睡好。

Pattern 2: S (已經) *how long* 没-V 了 (up to present or current relevance)

  b. 我已經三個晚上沒睡覺了。

Situations When V-了 Is Not Used

1. with non-action verbs: 是、叫、姓、愛、能、會、覺得、知道...

  a. 他們覺得 (x) 每天只有一個太陽飛到天上去太沒有意思了。

2. habitual/repeated actions (with adverbs 常常、每天、總是...)

  a. 去年我們常常到山上去玩兒 (x)。

3. verbs taking verbal constructions as their objects: 決定、開始、請、要、叫、...

  a. 他們決定 (x) 第二天一起飛到天上去。

4. speech verbs taking (in)direct speech as their objects: 說、問、告訴、聽說...

  a. 我問 (x) 爸爸我為甚麼不能有個弟弟？他說 (x) 一家只能有一個孩子。

就 and 才

就 (as early as) and 才 (not until, only after ... did ...) are both time-oriented adverbs, which should be placed only before a verb phrase. They are used to describe an action in a time frame. 就 focuses on the promptness of the action, relative to an *expected time* or another action; 才, on the other hand, focuses on the tardiness of the action. When 就 or 才 is used, one should make sure that time reference is provided. This reference takes the form of a time phrase or another action. In short, the promptness and tardiness of the action are relative to the *speaker's expectation*.

An affirmative sentence in Chinese that uses 才 as an adverb of time should be rendered as a negative sentence in English.

  Examples:

1. 她今天早上就來了。

  She had already come by this morning. (She came as early as this morning, more quickly than you expected)

2. 她今天早上才到。

  She didn't arrive until this morning. (You expected her to arrive earlier)

3. 我認識他以前就知道他家有很多孩子了。

  I knew that there were many kids in his family before I met him.

4. 我認識他以後才知道他家有很多孩子。

    I didn't know that there are many kids in his family until I met him.
    (Only after I met him did I know that there are many kids in his family.)

5. 我知道他很着急，我吃了飯馬上就去。

    I know he is anxious, so I'll go immediately after I eat.

6. 我太餓了，我得吃了飯才能去。

    I am too hungry. I won't be able to go until after I eat something.

句型和詞匯用法
SENTENCE PATTERNS AND WORD USAGE

Study the following examples and create a sentence using each phrase or pattern.

就是

1. 太陽從東方飛到西方，最後飛回樹上，這就是一天。
2. 他就是從上海來的那個人。
3. 兄弟就是哥哥跟弟弟。
4. 你現在問的問題就是我昨天要問的。
5. 他就是要跟我姐姐結婚的人。
6. _____。

覺得

1. 這十個太陽覺得每天只有一個飛到天上去沒有意思。
2. 我今天覺得很不舒服。
3. 我覺得他太喜歡玩了。
4. 你覺得他說的話有意思嗎?
5. 我覺得我們應該幫助他。
6. _____。

會

1. 如果人們看見天上有那麼多太陽，一定會很高興。
2. 我明年會住在北京。
3. 我想明天會下雨。
4. 他的朋友很會射箭。
5. 李名很會照顧老年人。
6. _____。

叫

1. 神非常生氣，就叫最會射箭的羿到地上來幫助人們。
2. 他長得很高大，我們都叫他大山。
3. 我哥哥叫我替他想一個主意。
4. 他媽媽叫他回家，不要在外頭玩，可是他不聽。
5. _____。

……(的) 時候

1. 古時候，天上有十個太陽。
2. 我小時候，最喜歡到山上去玩兒。
3. 天氣很冷的時候，住在這兒非常不舒服。
4. 我在北京的時候，去了很多有意思的地方。
5. _____。

一樣

1. 這十個太陽長得完全一樣。
2. 北方人吃的東西跟南方人吃的一樣嗎?
3. 這兩個地方的天氣很不一樣。
4. 每天做一樣的事情，太沒有意思了。
5. _____。

那麼(這麼)

1. 如果人們看見天上有那麼多太陽，一定會很高興。
2. 今天怎麼這麼熱? 是不是因為十個太陽都出來了?
3. 天氣這麼冷，你就不要到山上去了。
4. A: 她為甚麼總是那麼累? B: 因為她的孩子那麼多，又那麼小。
5. _____。

如果……(就)……

1. 如果人們看見天上有那麼多太陽，一定會很高興。
2. 如果你不知道這件事，就去問問他吧。
3. 如果明天下雪，我們就不去那兒了。
4. 如果上海的冬天和夏天天氣也很好，那我就想住到上海去。
5. _____。

練習
EXERCISES

語音漢字練習 Pronunciation and Characters

1. Write the pinyin romanization for the underlined characters.

   事<u>情</u>　　難<u>過</u>　　　　很<u>冷</u>　　　　<u>死</u>了

   <u>請</u>問　　老<u>人</u>　　　　可<u>能</u>　　　　<u>時</u>候

   <u>舒</u>服　　<u>昨</u>天　　　　就<u>是</u>　　　　馬<u>上</u>

   <u>睡</u>覺　　<u>住</u>在　　　　有意<u>思</u>　　　晚<u>上</u>

2. Write the characters for the following; pay special attention to the underlined syllable.

   shí<u>hou</u>　　　　　<u>nán</u>rén　　　　　dì<u>di</u>

   zuì<u>hòu</u>　　　　　<u>nán</u>guò　　　　　<u>dì</u>yītiān

   shè<u>jiàn</u>　　　　　<u>ná</u>dōngxi　　　　<u>zhī</u>dào

   kàn<u>jiàn</u>　　　　　<u>nǎ</u>er　　　　　　shēng<u>qì</u>

3. Write the meaning of the following radicals.

   木 _____　　亻 _____　　日 _____

4. Using the meaning of the radicals, guess the meaning of the following words. Match the translation to the characters. (Do not use a dictionary.)

   松樹_____　　　　a. the Milky Way

   晶_____　　　　b. pace up and down

   枇杷_____　　　　c. brilliant; glittering

   徘徊_____　　　　d. bridge

   星河_____　　　　e. dark

   橋_____　　　　f. loquat

   暗_____　　　　g. pine tree

詞匯練習 **Vocabulary Practice**

1. 選詞填空 (Fill in the blanks of the following dialogues or passages by selecting appropriate words from the list provided. Words can be used more than once.)

   (如果、就是、覺得、會、叫、時候、有意思、一樣、那麼、一共)

   1) A：從昨天到今天，我_____看了三本書，太累了。今天我_____很不舒服，所以不能跟你到中國城去買東西了。我想____我妹妹跟你一起去，可以嗎？

      B：沒有問題，你去和你妹妹去不是_____嗎？

   2) A：美國人跟中國人完全不_____嗎？

      B：我_____他們有的地方_____，有的地方不_____。

   3) A：你知道小王的女朋友是誰嗎？

      B：_____他左邊的那個女的。

      A：哇 (Wow)！我不知道小王有一個_____好看的女朋友！你知道他們甚麼_____結婚嗎？

      B：我想，小王有工作以後他們就_____結婚了吧。

   4) 中國人的名字很_____，一個人的名字可能_____他/她出生的地方，也可能是他/她出生的時間。比方說，_____一個女孩的名字____"海英"，她就可能是在上海生的；_____一個男孩叫"雪生"，那他出生的_____天上可能在下大雪。

2. 選擇填空 (Fill in the blanks.)
   1) 我要他今天來，可是他昨天____來了。　　a. 就　　b. 才　　c. 還
   2) 我要他昨天來，可是他今天____來。　　　a. 就　　b. 才　　c. 還
   3) 他____中國到美國來的時候，還不會說英文。　a. 去　　b. 到　　c. 從
   4) 我們家____有四個人：我父母、哥哥、和我。　a. 一共　b. 一定　c. 一起

5) 這個地方現在＿＿非常好看了。　　　　a. 長得　b. 變得　c. 覺得

6) 你現在問的問題＿＿我昨天要問的。　　a. 還是　b. 就　c. 就是

7) 我不＿＿小王的女朋友。　　　　　　　a. 知道　b. 認識　c. 會

8) 我不＿＿小王的女朋友是誰。　　　　　a. 知道　b. 認識　c. 會

9) 我不＿＿說中國話。　　　　　　　　　a. 知道　b. 認識　c. 會

10) 你不要着急，我＿＿幫助你的。　　　　a. 應該　b. 就　c. 會

語法練習 Grammar

1. Complete the following sentences, using 了 to indicate a change of state and *give the reason for the change*.

    e.g., 這個湖裏頭以前有很多魚，＿＿＿＿＿＿＿＿＿＿＿＿＿＿＿＿＿。
    → 這個湖裏頭以前有很多魚，<u>可是今年冬天太冷，湖裏的魚都死了</u>。

1) 張文以前很怕熱，＿＿＿＿＿＿＿＿＿＿＿＿＿＿＿＿＿＿＿＿＿＿。

2) 這個地方以前只有一所房子，＿＿＿＿＿＿＿＿＿＿＿＿＿＿＿＿＿。

3) 去年她在上海工作，＿＿＿＿＿＿＿＿＿＿＿＿＿＿＿＿＿＿＿＿。

4) 她結婚以前姓王，＿＿＿＿＿＿＿＿＿＿＿＿＿＿＿＿＿＿＿＿＿。

5) 中國以前有很多大家庭，＿＿＿＿＿＿＿＿＿＿＿＿＿＿＿＿＿＿。

6) 去年她來這兒的時候，沒有幾個朋友。＿＿＿＿＿＿＿＿＿＿＿＿。

7) 這件事以前我不知道，＿＿＿＿＿＿＿＿＿＿＿＿＿＿＿＿＿＿＿。

8) 小張以前愛吃魚，＿＿＿＿＿＿＿＿＿＿＿＿＿＿＿＿＿＿＿＿＿。

9) 昨天她很難過，_____。

10) 她以前不會說中國話，_____。

2. Insert 了 into each sentence in its appropriate positions to indicate "completion of an action."

1) 前天我給小王介紹一個女朋友。

2) 他父母去年給他很多錢，他都用。

3) 昨天我去他家的時候，經過一個很好看的小湖。

4) 上個月我在我妹妹家住兩天。

5) 中午我吃兩條魚，現在覺得很不舒服。

6) A：你今天看書嗎？ B：還沒呢。

綜合練習 Comprehensive Exercises

Helpful Vocabulary

早上	zǎoshang	morning
中午	zhōngwǔ	noon
離	lí	away from, to
近	jìn	close
遠	yuǎn	far

Read the following passage and fill in the blanks with appropriate words from the list.

(覺得、一樣、如果、那麼、了、知道、時候、看見、有意思、可是、所以)

　　有一天，兩個小孩在海邊說話。他們_____一位老人從前邊過來了，就對老人說："老爺爺，我們有一個問題，可以問問您嗎？" 老人說："好啊，甚麼問題啊？"男孩兒說："我＿＿＿＿太陽早上離我們近，＿＿＿＿她說太陽中午離我們近。您知道的事情多，您說太陽甚麼＿＿＿＿離我們近呢？"

老人對男孩說："這個問題很＿＿＿＿！你說說，你為甚麼覺得太陽早上離我們近呢？"男孩說："＿＿＿＿的東西，離我們近的時候大，離我們遠的時候小。早上的太陽非常大，＿＿＿＿我覺得早上的太陽離我們近。"老人又問那個女孩兒："那你為甚麼說中午的太陽離我們近呢？"女孩兒說："熱的東西＿＿＿＿離我們近，我們就覺得熱，可是離我們遠的時候我們就不覺得＿＿＿＿熱了。您看現在中午的太陽多熱，所以我說中午的太陽離我們近。"

老人聽了兩個孩子的話說："你們倆說的都對，現在我都不＿＿＿＿應該怎麼說＿＿＿＿"。

Answer the following questions according to the above passage.

1. 為甚麼那兩個小孩要問那位老人一個問題？

2. 男孩覺得太陽甚麼時候離我們近？為甚麼？

3. 女孩覺得太陽甚麼時候離我們近？為甚麼？

4. 老人覺得太陽甚麼時候離我們近？為甚麼？

寫作練習 Writing

Use 了 in appropriate situations (sentence-final 了 indicating change of state; or verb-suffix 了 indicating completion of an action or event) in writing the following two short essays.

1. "昨天": a short essay about your activities yesterday
2. "她/他變了": a short essay on anyone who you think has changed recently

閱讀練習 Reading Comprehension

Read the following passage quickly and answer the questions.

小文的 日記 (rìjì, diary)

五月一號, 星期二, 雨

  今天又下雨了, 已經下了幾天了, 真沒有意思。媽媽說我不能出去玩, 因為外頭下大雨, 太冷。可是張小妹為甚麼可以在外頭玩呢? 她媽媽多好呵。

  媽媽昨天給我講了一個故事 (jiǎng gùshi, tell a story), 她說很早以前天上有十個太陽。天變得非常熱, 很多人, 樹, 動物都死了。後來有一個叫羿的神, 從天上到地下來, 射下了九個太陽, 現在天上就只有一個太陽了。可是我覺得只有一個太陽也不好。每天只有它在天上飛, 太累了, 所以有的時候它要在樹上休息 (xiūxi, rest), 不出來。這幾天它一定是在樹上休息了。我希望天上有四個太陽, 一個在東方, 一個在西方, 一個在南方, 一個在北方, 這樣它們就不會太累, 每天都有一個太陽出來, 我也就可以天天在外頭玩了。

問題:

1. 小文的日記是哪一天寫的? 這天天氣怎麼樣?

2. 小文為甚麼不喜歡這樣的天氣?

3. 小文想今天的太陽到哪兒去了?

4. 為甚麼小文覺得應該有四個太陽?

5. 小文覺得只有一個太陽的時候有甚麼問題?

WORDS AND EXPRESSIONS ON SPECIFIC TOPICS
時間 (Time)

1.	前天	qiántiān	day before yesterday
2.	昨天	zuótiān	yesterday
3.	今天	jīntiān	today
4.	明天	míngtiān	tomorrow
5.	後天	hòutiān	day after tomorrow
6.	早上	zǎoshàng	morning
7.	中午	zhōngwǔ	noon
8.	下午	xiàwǔ	afternoon
9.	晚上	wǎnshàng	evening
10.	上個星期	shàngge xīngqī	last week
11.	這個星期	zhèige xīngqī	this week
12.	下個星期	xiàge xīngqī	next week
13.	上/這/下個月	shàng/zhè/xiàge yuè	last/this/next month
14.	去年	qùnián	last year
15.	今年	jīnnián	this year
16.	明年	míngnián	next year
17.	兩點鐘	liǎngdiǎnzhōng	2:00
18.	四點一刻	sìdiǎn yíkè	4:15
19.	三點十五分	sāndiǎn shíwǔ fēn	3:15
20.	五點半	wǔdiǎnbàn	5:30
21.	兩個鐘頭	liǎngge zhōngtóu	2 hours
22.	四個鐘頭/小時零十五分	sìge zhōngtóu/xiǎoshí líng shíwǔ fēn	4 hours and 15 minutes

WORDS AND EXPRESSIONS ON SPECIFIC TOPICS
時間 (Time) (*continued*)

23. 上午十點零五分	shàngwǔ shídiǎn líng wǔ fēn	10:05 a.m.
24. 下午六點半	xiàwǔ liùdiǎn bàn	6:30 p.m.
25. 一九九九年十月二十三號／日，星期六	yījiǔjiǔjiǔ nián shí yuè èrshísān hào/rì, xīngqī liù	Saturday, October 23, 1999

第五課. 天和地

Lesson 5. Heaven and Earth

Before You Read

Getting Started: Study the picture and discuss it.

1. 蛋裏頭和蛋外頭都有甚麼東西?

2. 太陽和月亮是甚麼東西變的?

生詞
VOCABULARY

1.	蛋	dàn	N	egg
2.	着	zhe	suffix	verb suffix indicating a durative state
3.	盤古	Pángǔ	PN	the name of the god who, according to legend, created the heaven and the earth
4.	醒	xǐng	V	to wake up
5.	睜開	zhēngkāi	VP	to open (one's eyes)
6.	眼睛	yǎnjīng	N	eye
7.	世界	shìjiè	N	the world
8.	黑	hēi	SV	black; dark
9.	踢	tī	V	to kick
10.	出來	chūlái	VP	to come out/to emerge
11.	輕	qīng	SV	light
12.	重	zhòng	SV	heavy
13.	乾淨	gānjìng	SV	clean
14.	慢	màn	SV	slow
15.	地	de	Pt.	adverbial marker
16.	上昇	shàngshēng	VP	to rise
17.	變成	biànchéng	VP	to become; to change into
18.	下沉	xiàchén	VP	to sink
19.	分開	fēnkāi	VP	to separate; to part
20.	站着	zhànzhe	VP	to be standing
21.	厚	hòu	SV	thick
22.	身體	shēntǐ	N	body
23.	過	guò	V	to pass; to spend (time)

24. 又	yòu	Adv.	again
25. 氣	qì	N	breath; air; gas
26. 風	fēng	N	wind
27. 雲	yún	N	cloud
28. 聲音	shēngyīn	N	voice; sound
29. 雷	léi	N	thunder
30. 月亮	yuèliang	N	moon
31. 手	shǒu	N	hand
32. 腳	jiǎo	N	foot
33. 頭髮	tóufa	N	hair
34. 樹木	shùmù	N	tree
35. 血	xiě, xuè	N	blood
36. 汗	hàn	N	sweat; perspiration
37. 新	xīn	SV	new
38. 久	jiǔ	SV	long (time)
39. 最近	zuìjìn	TW	recent
40. 聰明	cōngming	SV	intelligent; bright
41. 怎麼樣	zěnmeyàng	IE	How are things? How about . . . ?
42. 不錯	búcuò	SV	pretty good
43. 別的	biéde	Pron.	other; alternative
44. 行	xíng	SV	okay

First Reading: Getting the Main Ideas

Read the following story quickly and indicate the main ideas based on the text. The second one is provided.

1. _____。
2. 盤古死了以後，他的身體變成了一個新世界。

天和地

很久以前，沒有天和地，只有一個很大的蛋。蛋裏頭睡着一個叫盤古的神。盤古在那個蛋裏睡了一萬八千年。

有一天，盤古睡醒了，他睜開眼睛，想看看世界是甚麼樣子。可是蛋裏很黑，甚麼也看不見。盤古用力一踢，蛋破了，從裏頭流出來了很多東西。這些東西有的輕有的重，有的乾淨有的不乾淨。那些輕的、乾淨的東西慢慢地上升，變成了天。那些重的、不乾淨的東西，慢慢地下沉，變成了地。

天和地分開以後，盤古就在天和地的中間站着。天一天一天地變高；地一天一天地變厚；盤古的身體也一天一天地變高變大。又過了一萬八千年，天和地不變了，這時候盤古就死了。

盤古死了以後，他的氣變成了風和雲，他的聲音變成了雷，他的眼睛變成了太陽和月亮。他的手、腳和身體變成了大山小山。他的頭髮變成了樹木，他的血變成了河，他的汗變成了雨。盤古死了，可是他的身體變成了一個新世界。

Second Reading: Getting the Specific Information

Reread the story carefully and indicate whether the following statements are true or false. Write "T" for true and "F" for false.

___ 1. 很久以前，在天和地中間有一個很大的蛋。
___ 2. 盤古在蛋裏頭睡了一萬八千年。
___ 3. 他睡醒以後很生氣，因為蛋裏很黑。
___ 4. 蛋自己破了，盤古就出來了。
___ 5. 盤古出來以後，變成了天和地。
___ 6. 盤古變了幾年以後就死了。
___ 7. 盤古死了以後，他的眼睛變成了太陽和月亮。
___ 8. 盤古的身體變成了一個新世界。

Understanding the Text Structure

1. Put these events in the story in order by number.

   _____ 盤古在蛋裏睡了一萬八千年。

   _____ 盤古死了以後，他的身體變成了一個新世界。

   _____ 很久以前沒有天和地，只有一個很大的蛋。

   _____ 盤古在天和地的中間站着。

   _____ 盤古睡醒了以後要從蛋裏出來，所以就用腳踢破了那個蛋。

   _____ 蛋破了，流出來了很多東西，這些東西變成了天和地。

2. The characterization of a typical story structure can be divided into six categories: setting, event, response, attempt at action, consequence, and reaction. Of course, most stories have more than one event, and not all six categories are included in all stories. This lesson has four events, connected by means of time expressions. In the following exercises:

- Identify the time expressions that connect the four events.

   _____

   _____

   _____

   _____

- Analyze the first two paragraphs according to the story structure categories given above.

   Setting (the protagonist and the place) _____

   _____

   Event _____

   _____

---

86   Lesson 5. Heaven and Earth

Response of the protagonist _____

_____

Attempt to do what? _____

_____

Consequence _____

會話
DIALOGUE

(Gao is the former classmate of Sun's elder sister. Gao is asking Sun about her elder sister.)

高：很久沒見到你姐姐了，她最近怎麼樣?

孫：她最近很忙，就要結婚了。

高：噢，我知道她的男朋友是誰。他長得不錯，叫張華，對不對?

孫：不對，那是她以前的男朋友。

高：甚麼?她跟張華分開了!為甚麼?

孫：因為我姐姐不愛他了。

高：以前你姐姐不是跟他很好嗎?怎麼不愛他了?

孫：因為他跟別的女孩子好了。

高：噢……，你姐姐現在的男朋友怎麼樣?

孫：他很聰明，人也很好。長得嘛……，還行。

Practice: Find a partner to talk about the recent changes in your (or someone else') life.

語法介紹
GRAMMATICAL POINTS

The Use of 了 in Discourse

In the previous lesson, we learned that 了 conveys the meaning of "change of state", or "completion" / "accomplishment" of a single action/event in a sentence. However, in daily life people seldom communicate in single sentences. More often they conduct discourse, which shows a series of connected events and states intertwined. It is the discourse function of 了 that is discussed in this lesson.

A discourse, in general, consists of a series of segments representing events, situations, and conditions. Among these segments there are one or two prominent events supported by other minor events or situations. A major discourse function of 了 is to mark these prominent events. It is therefore very important to note that in a long stretch of discourse not *every* action verb in past events will take 了 (except in some obligatory contexts such as verb-了 with quantified objects or verbs such as 死, 破, etc.). When to use 了 in the discourse depends on whether the speaker views a verb as representing the action of the prominent event(s) of the discourse.

Compare the following two sentences:

(1) 昨天我到中國城去了。

(2) 昨天我到中國城去(x)，買了很多東西。

In sentence (1), 昨天我到中國城去了 is a simple completed event. However, in sentence (2) this event is used to provide the circumstance of the main action: 買了很多東西, so 了 is not used for the first event. If we use 了, we then break it into two separate events. An example from the text further illustrates the point.

有一天，盤古睡醒了，	(main event)
他睜開眼睛，	(subsequent event 1)
想看看世界是甚麼樣子。	(subsequent event 2)
可是蛋裏很黑，他甚麼也看不見。	(subsequent event 3)
盤古用力一踢，	(subsequent event 4)
蛋破了，從裏頭流出來很多東西。	(closing event)

In this piece of narrative, "盤古 woke up" is the main event because all the subsequent events were related to this one. But the series of actions 盤古 did after he woke up, opened his eyes, tried to look at the world, couldn't see anything, and kicked the egg . . . were not all distinctive until "the egg broke," which marks the ending of this series. Moreover, "break" is a verb that indicates a very brief action with a "built-in terminal point." Thus, in narrative discourse, only the main event(s) will be marked by 了. The other verb phrases describing the circumstances or related sequences of events do not necessarily take 了. If 了 is used, it breaks the sequence into separate steps. For example, we could add a 了 in the sentence 他睜開眼睛 (to make it 他睜開了眼睛). However, without it, the sequence will flow more smoothly.

Here is another example from the text.

天和地分開以後，	(circumstance of the event--time)
盤古就在天和地的中間站著。	(continuous state)
天一天一天地變高；	(continuous process)
地一天一天地變厚；	(continuous process)
盤古的身體也一天一天地變高變大。	(continuous process)
又過了一萬八千年，	(quantified object)
天和地不變了，	(change of state)
這時候盤古就死了。	(main event/completion)

Action Verb and Complements of Result—Resultative Verb Phrase

The function of a Chinese action verb is only to name an action. It thus is void of result. In English an action verb, in contrast, often has embedded in it the result of the action. For example, the English verb "to see" has the concept of "to look, resulting in perceiving." Consequently, in order to express the idea of "the action and its result" in Chinese, one must use the construction "verb + result." This structure is difficult to learn because there are many resultative complements in Chinese. Moreover, it is not easy to grasp the implications of these complements. The way to master this structure is to learn a few at a time and to internalize them. This lesson introduces just a few.

- 醒	awaken		- 出來	out; emerge
- 開	open		- 成	into

There are two types of resultative verb phrases.

Actual Type

The semantic implication of this structure, "verb + result," is that an action happened and it did or did not produce the expected result.

V + resultative ending + 了　　　　沒 + V + resultative ending
(the result has been achieved)　　　(no result has been achieved)

睡醒了	woke up	沒睡醒	did not wake up
睜開了	opened (eyes)	沒睜開	did not open
流出來了	flowed out	沒流出來	did not flow out
看見了	saw	沒看見	did not see

她睡醒了，不想再睡了。

她睡醒了，可是還沒睜開眼睛。

蛋破了，流出來很多東西。

Potential Type

The structure indicates that an action is going to take place and the action can/could or cannot/could not produce the expected result.

V + 得 + resultative ending　　　　　　V + 不 + resultative ending
(action able to produce result)　　　　　(action not able to produce result)

睜得開	can/could open (eyes)	睜不開	cannot/could not open eyes
看得見	can/could see	看不見	cannot/could not see
流得出來	can/could flow out	流不出來	cannot/could not flow out

蛋破了，可是東西流不出來。

天黑了，你看得見看不見那個人?

那邊有一棵很高的樹，你看得見嗎?

我醒了，可是睜不開眼睛。

句型和詞匯用法
SENTENCE PATTERNS AND WORD USAGE

Study the following examples and create a sentence using each phrase or pattern.

地

1. 那些輕的、乾淨的東西就慢慢地上升，變成了天。
2. 老張很生氣地說："請你出去!"
3. 孩子一天天地長大了。
4. 王中和他女朋友分開了，他難過地說以後再也不找女朋友了。
5. _____。

A 變成 B

1. 盤古死了以後，他的氣變成了風和雲，他的聲音變成了雷。
2. 小明以前很不聽話，現在變成了一個很聽話的孩子了。
3. 以前這是一個小地方，現在變成一個大城市了。
4. _____。

過

1. 他說他要給我介紹一個女朋友，已經過了三天了，他還沒給我介紹。
2. 過了很久我才知道他不會用電腦。
3. 明天我過生日，請你來我家吃飯好嗎?
4. 我父親決定今年到南方去過冬天，因為這兒冬天太冷。
5. _____。

結婚

1. 你覺得李東的這位女朋友會跟他結婚嗎?
2. 他們結婚四年了，還沒有孩子。
3. 張英的父母很着急，因為她今年三十歲了還沒結婚。
4. _____。

練習
EXERCISES

語音漢字練習 Pronunciation and Characters

1. Write the pinyin romanization for the following characters.

很<u>輕</u>	<u>分</u>開	<u>流</u>出來	頭<u>髮</u>
<u>經</u>過	大<u>風</u>	<u>樓</u>房	說<u>話</u>
天<u>神</u>	最<u>近</u>	下<u>沉</u>	新<u>朋</u>友
<u>聲</u>音	乾<u>淨</u>	變<u>成</u>	<u>醒</u>來

2. Write the characters for the following; pay special attention to the underlined syllables.

<u>shēn</u>tǐ	<u>fēi</u>cháng	liú<u>xiě</u>
<u>shēng</u>qì	<u>fēi</u>dào	xià<u>xuě</u>
<u>shǒu</u>jiǎo	hěn<u>hòu</u>	<u>shì</u>jiè
hěn<u>shǎo</u>	<u>hòu</u>lái	<u>shì</u>qing

3. Write the meaning of the following radicals.

貝 _____

門 _____

扌 _____

4. Using the meaning of the radicals, guess the meaning of the following words. Match the translation to the characters. (Do not use a dictionary.)

投擲 _____   a. attic; loft

Lesson 5. Heaven and Earth   93

貪心_____ b. carry water (on a shoulder pole)

閣樓_____ c. greedy

挑水_____ d. close a door

關門_____ e. throw; fling

資財_____ f. capital goods; assets

詞匯和語法練習 Vocabulary and Grammar

1. Fill in the blanks with an appropriate word.

1) 小王喜歡用左手_____東西。

2) 你不應該用腳_____那個小動物。

3) 輕的東西慢慢地_____ _____，重的東西慢慢地_____ _____。

4) 每個人都應該用自己的眼睛_____世界。

5) 那個孩子看_____他媽媽以後，很高興。

6) 有太陽的時候，奶奶的眼睛就睜不_____。

7) 現在北方的一些大城市很不_____淨。

8) 今天真熱，我_____了很多汗。

9) 天上沒有月亮，所以外頭很_____。

10) 我很_____沒有看見你姐姐了，她最近好嗎?

2. Fill in the blanks with 了 where it is necessary:

1) 明天是小張太太的生日_____，小張覺得現在應該去_____城裏給他太太買個東西_____。決定_____以後，小張就開車_____到城裏去_____。不知道為甚麼，城裏的人非常多。小張一共去_____四家店 (diàn, shop)，都沒有看見_____他喜歡的東西。天要黑_____的時候，小張在第五家店裏看見_____一件很好看的毛衣 (máoyī, sweater) _____。他馬上就買_____。

小張回到家裏的時候，天已經完全黑____。

2) 他以前不喜歡在外面睡_____，現在喜歡_____。今天他在房子前頭的草地上睡_____很久。睡醒_____以後，看見_____一只小羊在他的身邊吃_____草。

3. Fill in the blanks with appropriate resultative verb phrases provided.

看見了　　沒看見　　看得見　　看不見　　睜開了　　沒睜開　　睜得開
睜不開　　流出來　　沒流出來　　流得出來　　流不出來

1) 昨天我在城裏_____一個很奇怪的人。

2) 我睡醒了，可是_____眼睛，因為我太累了。

3) 蛋破了，_____很多東西，可是我不知道這些東西是甚麼。

4) 那邊很高的山上站着一個小孩子，你_____嗎?

5) 屋子裏很黑，我睡醒了，睜開眼睛，可是_____東西。

6) 蛋破了，可是破的地方很小，所以裏頭的東西都_____。

綜合練習 Comprehensive Exercises

Fill in the blanks with words provided.

時間　出生　事情　應該　認識　長得　結婚　聰明　北部　決定

老高是在美國_____的，他_____很高，很好看，人也很_____。現在老高在美國_____的一個大城市工作。他工作很忙，每天都有很多_____要做，所以他常說自己不應該_____，因為他沒有_____。老高每天回家以後就睡，睡醒了就去工作。最近他_____不能再這麼工作了，他覺得自己太累了，_____

休息了。他也希望能用休息的時間_____一些新朋友，找到 (zhǎodào, find) 一個想跟他結婚的人。

口語練習 Oral Exercise

Discussion: Give your opinion on the creation of the earth.

寫作練習 Writing

Write an essay describing a person using as many of the following words or expressions as possible.

最近/結婚/眼睛/乾淨/身體/站/慢/聰明/聲音/頭髮/手/腳/睡/醒

閱讀練習 Reading Comprehension

Read the following passage quickly and answer the questions.

女媧 (Nǚwā) 造人

很久以前，天上有太陽，月亮，雲；地上有山，河，樹，還有一些動物，可是沒有人。地上只住着一個女神，叫女媧。女媧覺得這個世界很好：天高高的，天上有太陽和月亮，有時候還有幾塊雲，非常好看；地上有山、有樹、有河，還有很多可愛的小動物。女媧很喜歡這些小動物，因為這些動物都是她的朋友。女媧給每個動物都起了一個很好聽的名字。在這個世界上，女媧覺得非常高興。

有一天，女媧在草地上跟一些小動物玩，玩累了以後，她就到一條小河邊去看河裏的魚。女媧看魚的時候，看見水裏有一位好看的姑娘，她很高興，就對水裏的姑娘笑。她笑的時候，水裏的姑娘也笑；她用手打水的時候，水裏的姑娘也用手打水。最後女媧才知道水裏的姑娘就是她自己。她想，如果這個世界上也有跟她一樣的動物，一定會很有意思。所以她就用泥 (ní, mud) 做了一些跟她一樣的小人。小泥人到了地上以後，就開始笑了，也會說話了。從那個時候開始，世界上就有了人。

問題：

1. 女媧是誰？她住在哪兒？

2. 女媧為甚麼覺得很高興？

3. 在女媧的世界裏有甚麼，沒有甚麼？

4. 有一天，女媧在河邊看魚的時候看見了甚麼？

5. 她看見了水裏的東西以後決定做甚麼？

WORDS AND EXPRESSIONS ON SPECIFIC TOPICS
天氣 (Weather)

1.	陰天	yīntiān	cloudy day; overcast sky
2.	晴天	qíngtiān	sunny day
3.	冷	lěng	cold
4.	熱	rè	hot
5.	暖和	nuǎnhuo	warm
6.	涼快	liángkuai	pleasantly cool
7.	刮風	guāfēng	wind blowing
8.	打雷	dǎléi	to thunder
9.	下雨	xiàyǔ	to rain
10.	下雪	xiàxuě	to snow
11.	四季	sìjì	the four seasons
12.	春天	chūntiān	spring
13.	夏天	xiàtiān	summer
14.	秋天	qiūtiān	autumn
15.	冬天	dōngtiān	winter

第六課. 成語故事

Lesson 6. The Story of Chinese Idioms

Before You Read

Getting Started: Study the pictures and discuss them.

1. 那位音樂家在做甚麼?
2. 那幾個人在畫甚麼? 他們為甚麼要畫?
3. 你知道成語是甚麼嗎? 你會說多少成語?

生詞
VOCABULARY

1.	成語	chéngyǔ	N	idiom; set phrase
2.	故事	gùshi	N	story
3.	對	duì	CV	toward; to
4.	彈琴	tánqín	VO	play the zither
5.	音樂	yīnyuè	N	music
6.	音樂家	yīnyuèjiā	N	musician
7.	得	de	Pt.	verb complement marker
8.	帶	dài	V	to bring
9.	頭	tóu	N/M	head/ measure word for animals
10.	它	tā	Pron.	it
11.	曲子	qǔzi	N	tune, melody
12.	好像	hǎoxiàng	Adv.	as if; seemingly
13.	越……越……	yuè…yuè…	Conj.	the more . . . the more
14.	一點(兒)	yìdiǎn(r)	N	a little
15.	興趣	xìngqù	N	interest
16.	懂	dǒng	V	to understand; to comprehend
17.	別人	biérén	N	other people, others
18.	笨	bèn	SV	stupid
19.	畫	huà	V/N	to draw; to paint; painting; picture
20.	蛇	shé	N	snake; serpent
21.	添	tiān	V	to add
22.	足	zú	N	foot
23.	喝	hē	V	to drink

24.	酒	jiǔ	N	wine; alcohol; liquor
25.	得到	dédào	V	to get; to obtain; to gain
26.	瓶	píng	N/M	bottle
27.	不得了	bùdéliǎo	IE	extremely; terribly; awfully
28.	當然	dāngrán	Adv.	of course
29.	夠	gòu	SV/Adv.	enough
30.	快	kuài	SV	fast; quick
31.	極了	jíle	IE	extremely
32.	本來	běnlái	Adv.	originally; essentially
33.	連……都……	lián…dōu…	IE	even
34.	雖然	suīrán	Conj.	although, though
35.	說明	shuōmíng	V	to illustrate; to show; to indicate
36.	必要	bìyào	SV/N	necessary; necessity
37.	好處	hǎochù	N	good; benefit; advantage
38.	年輕	niánqīng	SV	young
39.	老大爺	lǎodàye	N	a respectful address for an elderly man
40.	急	jí	SV	urgent
41.	楚國	Chǔguó	PN	one of the Warring States (770–256 B.C.)
42.	誒	éi	Interj.	Hey!
43.	停	tíng	V	to stop
44.	馬	mǎ	N	horse
45.	車	chē	N	vehicle, car
46.	馬車	mǎ chē	N	chariot; (horse-drawn) carriage
47.	趕	gǎn	V	to drive (a horse or a chariot)
48.	路	lù	N	road

49. 不要緊	búyàojǐn	IE	It doesn't matter; Never mind
50. 跑	pǎo	V	to run
51. 哎呀	āiyā	Interj.	expressing complaint or impatience
52. 簡直	jiǎnzhí	Adv.	simply
53. 糊塗	hútu	SV	muddled; confused; bewildered
54. 道理	dàolǐ	N	reason
55. 離	lí	CV	away from
56. 遠	yuǎn	SV	far; distant

> **First Reading**: Getting the Main Ideas
>
> Two Chinese idioms are introduced in this text. Each idiom has a main idea. Read the text and choose the statement that best summarizes the main idea for each idiom.
>
> 成語(一) a.對別人說他聽不懂的話就是對牛彈琴。
>
> b.對牛彈琴就是說應該給牛彈好聽的音樂的意思。
>
> 成語(二) a.畫蛇畫得快的人應該給蛇畫上腳。
>
> b.給本來沒有腳的蛇畫上腳沒有必要，也沒有好處。

(一) 對牛彈琴

很久以前，有一位音樂家，他彈琴彈得非常好，大家都喜歡聽。有一天，天氣很好，他想，"今天到外頭去彈琴一定很有意思。"他就帶上琴到城外去了。他看見一頭牛在草地上吃草，就給它彈起了很好聽的曲子。他彈了很久，可是那頭牛還是低頭吃草，好像沒聽見。

音樂家越想越生氣。為甚麼這頭牛對他的音樂沒有一點興趣呢？是他彈得還不夠好聽嗎？人們對他說："你不要生氣了。不是你彈得不好，是牛不懂音樂，對它彈琴沒有用啊！"

現在如果有人對別人說他們聽不懂的話，人們就會說這個說話的人是在"對牛彈琴"。有時候人們也用這個成語來說有的人很笨，聽不懂別人說的話。

(二) 畫蛇添足

有一天，四個喜歡喝酒的人得到了一瓶酒。他們高興得不得了。可是，這一瓶酒四個人喝，當然不夠。張三說，"我們來畫蛇吧！誰畫得最快，這瓶酒就給誰喝。"大家都說這是一個好主意，就馬上開始畫蛇了。

張三第一個畫好了。他高興極了，說："你們畫得真慢！你看，我還有時間畫蛇腳呢。"他一邊說，一邊就開始畫蛇腳。這時候，李四也畫好了。他馬上拿起酒瓶，喝了一大口。張三很生氣，說："你不能喝！這瓶酒是我的！"李四一邊喝，一邊說，"對不起，這酒應該是我的。因為蛇本來沒有腳，你給它畫上腳，它就不是蛇了。"張三氣得連話都說不出來了。

張三雖然畫得很快，可是沒有得到這瓶酒。從這以後，人們就用"畫蛇添足"這個成語來說明做不必要的事情沒有好處。

Second Reading: Getting the Specific Information

Reread the text and indicate whether the following statements are true or false. If the statement is false, correct it.

對牛彈琴

____ 1. 因為天氣很好，所以這位音樂家想到城外去給牛彈琴。
____ 2. 牛喜歡吃草，可是對音樂沒有興趣。
____ 3. 牛對音樂沒有興趣，是因為這位音樂家彈琴彈得不够好。
____ 4. 音樂家很不高興，因為牛不懂音樂。
____ 5. 對别人説他聽不懂的話，就是對牛彈琴。

畫蛇添足

____ 6. 四個愛喝酒的人得到了一瓶酒，很高興，因為他們可以喝很多酒了。
____ 7. 大家都説張三的主意好得不得了。
____ 8. 雖然張三的主意很好，可是他畫蛇畫得不快。
____ 9. 如果張三能第一個畫好蛇腳，他就能得到那瓶酒了。
____10. 做沒有必要的事，説沒有必要的話，就是畫蛇添足。

Understanding the Text Structure

This lesson introduces some popular Chinese idioms —成語, which epitomize Chinese history and culture. It is usually difficult to translate these idioms into English literally. However, appropriate application of idioms in speaking and writing can greatly enhance the vividness and effectiveness of your expression. The typical features of 成語 are:

- Form: condensed four-character set phrase
- Meaning: usually derived from a (historical) story
- Use: metaphorical implication for vividness and effectiveness of expression

1. Fill in the blanks by summarizing the information from the text (in Chinese).

   a. 成語: 對牛彈琴

   Story: _____

   _____

   Implication: _____

   b. 成語: 畫蛇添足

   Story: _____

   _____

   Implication: _____

2. Use the appropriate idioms to complete the following sentences.

   a. 他一點兒也不懂電腦，跟他說電腦真的是_____。
   b. 該說的你都已經說了，再多說就是_____了。

Practice: Talk with a partner, using V得 and SV得 structures

(e.g., 長得……，聰明得……，糊塗得……，做事做得……，跑得……).

1. Describe a person you know (a friend, family member, etc.)
2. Ask questions about the person your partner described to you to get more information.

會話
DIALOGUE

(A long time ago, a young man met an old man while driving a chariot along a road.)

年輕人： 老大爺，您好！

老人： 你好啊，年輕人！這麽早，去哪兒啊？

年輕人： 我有一件急事，要到楚國去。

老人： 誒！停下來！停下來！楚國在南邊，可是你的馬車為甚麽往北走啊？

年輕人： 沒關係，我趕車趕得很好。

老人： 雖然你趕車趕得很好，可是這條路不去楚國啊！

年輕人： 不要緊。我錢帶得很多。

老人： 你錢帶得多又有甚麽用呢？這條路真的不去楚國啊！

年輕人： 沒問題。我的馬跑得快極了。

老人： 哎呀！跟你說話簡直就像對牛彈琴！你怎麽糊塗得連這個道理都不懂呢？你知道嗎？你的馬跑得越快，你離楚國就越遠了！

Indicate whether the following statements are true or false according to the dialogue.

____ 1. 年輕人的馬車在往南走，因為他想到南方的楚國去。

____ 2. 雖然年輕人趕車趕得很好，他到不了(cannot arrive) 楚國。

____ 3. 年輕人聽不懂老人的話。

____ 4. 老人很生氣，因為他覺得年輕人的馬跑得太快。

____ 5. 只有糊塗人才會做跟目的 (mùdì, goal) 相反(xiāngfǎn, opposite) 的事。

語法介紹
GRAMMATICAL POINTS

The Particle 得

得 can link a verb and its complement to comment on the performance of the action, that is, on the extent, effect, achievement, or quality attained by the verb. Very often such a complement in Chinese would be an adverbial expression in English.

Form:	S	V de	(adv.)	SV
	張三	畫得	(很)	快。
	你們	走得	(真)	慢。

Complements must directly follow the verb. Where there is an object after the verb (e.g., a VO compound), it is necessary to repeat the verb after the VO construction.

Form:	S	V O V	de	(adv.)	SV
	他	彈琴彈	得	(非常)	好。
	他們	喝酒喝	得	(不)	多。

Note 1: In this pattern, the first verb can be omitted. For example:

他(彈)琴彈得非常好。

他們(喝)酒喝得很多。

Note 2: It is also possible to put the object at the beginning of the sentence, to form a topic-comment structure. For example:

錢我帶得很多；東西我帶得不多。

中國菜你做得怎麼樣？

這張畫他畫得非常好。

得 can also link an SV and its complement of (intensifying) degree.

Form:	S	SV	de	degree
	他們	高興	得	不得了。
	這個主意	好	得	很。
	他	氣	得	連話都說不出來了。

句型和詞彙用法
SENTENCE PATTERNS AND WORD USAGE

Study the following examples and create a sentence using each phrase or pattern.

一邊......一邊......

1. 他一邊說，就一邊開始畫蛇腳。
2. 他一邊喝，一邊說。
3. 我爸爸喜歡一邊聽音樂，一邊喝酒。
4. _____。

越......越......

This pattern, often found in the form "越A越B," shows that B changes according to what A does. This usage has two types.

Type 1. The Subject of A Is Different from That of B.
1. 你的馬跑得越快，你就離楚國越遠了。
2. 老師越說，我越不懂。
3. 我越着急，他越不着急。
4. _____。

Type 2. A and B Share the Same Subject.
1. 音樂家越想越生氣。
2. 他越說越高興。
3. 你的話我越聽越糊塗。
4. _____。

連......也/都

The coverb 連 (even) is often used together with a coherent adverb such as 也 or 都. It introduces a noun/phrase for emphasis.

1. 他氣得連話也說不出來了。
2. 你怎麼連這個道理都不懂呢?

3. 這個字簡單得連我的小妹妹都會寫。

4. _____。

對……(沒)有興趣

1. 為甚麼牛對我的音樂沒有一點興趣啊?
2. 我哥哥從小就對畫畫兒有興趣。
3. 我喜歡聽音樂，可是對學音樂沒有甚麼興趣。
4. _____。

本來

1. 蛇本來沒有腳，你給它畫上腳，就不是蛇了。
2. 他本來身體不太好，後來天天跑步(pǎobù, jogging)，身體就好了。
3. 本來我不太想去，可是他一定要我去，我就去了。
4. _____。

雖然……可是……

Note: 雖然 can be used before or after the subject, but 可是 is generally at the very beginning of the clause.

1. 張三雖然畫得很快，可是沒有得到那瓶酒。
2. 他雖然字寫得不太好，可是中文說得很不錯。
3. 雖然我很想去，可是今天沒有時間，不能去。
4. _____。

簡直

1. 哎呀! 跟你說話簡直就是對牛彈琴!
2. 我簡直不知道他在說些甚麼!
3. 她非常喜歡畫畫。要是一張畫沒畫好，她簡直連覺也睡不著。
4. _____。

練習
EXERCISES

語音練習 Pronunciation

1. Write the pinyin romanization for the underlined characters.

很<u>少</u>	長<u>得</u>	<u>哪</u>兒	<u>得</u>到
老老<u>少</u>少	很<u>長</u>	<u>那</u>兒	覺<u>得</u>
<u>曲</u>子	好<u>像</u>	彈<u>琴</u>	興<u>趣</u>
<u>出</u>去	馬<u>上</u>	事<u>情</u>	好<u>處</u>

2. Write the characters for the following; pay special attention to the underlined syllables.

<u>měi</u>ge	<u>míng</u>zi	xìng<u>míng</u>
<u>Měi</u>guó	shuo<u>míng</u>	gāo<u>xìng</u>
<u>zài</u>nǎr	<u>nán</u>fāng	hǎo<u>jí</u>le
<u>zài</u>jiàn	<u>nán</u>rén	zháo<u>jí</u>

漢字練習 Chinese Characters

1. Indicate the radicals of the following characters, and look up their meaning.

　　a. 吃　喝　呢　啊　嗎　吧　　　(部首：____ 意思：_____)

　　b. 腳　腦　育　朋　　　　　　　(部首：____ 意思：_____)

　　c. 跑　跟　踢　路　　　　　　　(部首：____ 意思：_____)

2. Using the meaning of the radicals, guess the meaning of the following words. Match the meaning to the character. (Do not use a dictionary.)

胃	_____	a. horse hoof
跳	_____	b. the stomach
召	_____	c. to jump
美味	_____	d. fat, chubby
馬蹄	_____	e. to summon, call
胖	_____	f. finely flavored things, delicious

3. Which other characters have the same radicals?

_____

詞匯練習 Vocabulary Practice

1. Fill in the blanks with the appropriate words from the following list.

| 對牛彈琴 | 生氣 | 畫蛇添足 | 馬上 | 本來 |
| 雖然……可是 | 一邊……一邊…… | 對……有興趣 | 越……越…… | |

1) 我妹妹喜歡_____看書，_____聽音樂。

2) 他_____想學英文，可是聽說學中文很有用，就來我們大學學中文了。

3) 他_____學_____覺得中文的成語有意思。

4) 昨天我們到城外去玩兒了一天。回來的時候，_____我們都很累了，_____大家都很高興。

5) 她只喜歡音樂，_____電腦沒_____。

6) 別著急。我_____就來。

7) 這張畫很好看，再加顏色 (jiā yánsè, add colors) 就是_____了。

8) 小李的朋友都不想幫助他，所以他非常_____。

9) 我說過我不懂中國成語。你跟我說這些成語簡直是_____！

2. Select from the choices to complete the following sentences.

1) 今天的天氣好___，我們去城外吧。　　　　a. 不得了　b. 極了　　c. 很好

2) 雖然張三___得很快，可是没得到那瓶酒。　a. 畫蛇　　b. 畫蛇畫　c. 畫畫

3) 她的中國話說得___。　　　　　　　　　a. 不得了　b. 極了　　c. 好極了

4) 昨天雨___得我們不能出去。　　　　　　a. 太大　　b. 大　　　c. 很大

5) 她___說___高興，連上課都不想去了。　a. 越/越　　b. 多/多　　c. 又/又

6) 這個人___得連自己的生日都不知道是哪天。a. 聰明　　b. 着急　　c. 糊塗

7) 今天熱得___。　　　　　　　　　　　　a. 不得了　b. 極了　　c. 很熱

8) 世界上___沒有路，走的人多了，就成了路。a. 後來　　b. 本來　　c. 看來

3. Rewrite the following sentences, using the sentence patterns provided.

1) 張三很生氣，說不出話來了。(連......都......)

2) 這個字很簡單，我小妹妹都會寫。(連......都......)

3) 這個人真糊塗！他不知道自己住在哪兒。(連......都......)

4) 她不是中國人，也會說中國話。(雖然......可是......)

5) 這本書很有用，只是貴了一點兒。(雖然......可是......)

6) 我朋友很喜歡中國畫。(對......有興趣)

7) 要是你想學彈琴，我可以教你。(對......有興趣)

語法練習 Grammar

1. Fill in the blanks with the verbs provided and appropriate complements according to the context given. (Pay special attention to the VO structure.)

   e.g., 這個小孩_____, 大家都喜歡他。(長)

   → 這個小孩<u>長得很可愛</u>, 大家都喜歡他。

   1) 他_____, 沒人想坐他開的車。(開車)

   2) 昨天晚上她_____, 所以今天很累。(睡)

   3) 我朋友_____, 不少人都以為他是中國人。(說中文)

   4) 這棵樹_____, 今年好像還是去年那麼高。(長)

   5) 他昨天晚上_____, 所以今天不舒服。(喝酒)

   6) 這張畫_____, 誰也不喜歡。(畫)

   7) 我們對他的音樂沒有甚麼興趣, 因為他_____。(彈琴)

   8) 你們昨天去城外, _____? (玩)

寫作練習 Writing

Write about someone you like using the following words or expressions (use as many as you can). Indicate why you like him/her. Call your essay <u>我最喜歡的一個人</u>.

長得/ 畫畫兒畫得……/對……有興趣/雖然……可是/簡直/喝酒/彈琴/音樂/快/好處/問題/道理

閱讀練習 Reading Comprehension

Helpful Vocabulary

自相矛盾　　　　　zì xiāng máo dùn　　　　　self-contradictory

賣	mài	sell
武器	wǔqì	weapon
矛	máo	spear
盾	dùn	shield
結實	jiēshi	strong
刺穿	cì chuān	pierce through
剛才	gāngcái	just now

Read the following passage quickly.

自相矛盾

　　有一天，楚國的一個小城裏來了一個賣武器的人。他的矛和盾做得很好，很多人都過來看。賣武器的人拿起他的矛，對人們說，"你們看，我的矛是世界上最好的矛，連最結實的盾都能刺穿。"大家聽了他的話，都開始對他的矛有興趣了，可是只有人看，沒有人買。賣武器的人想，"沒人買我的矛，那我就賣盾吧。"

他就又拿起他的盾，對大家說，"看啊，這是世界上最結實的盾，連最好的矛也刺不穿它。"

　　有一個年輕人問，"你剛才說你的矛好得不得了，連最結實的盾也刺得穿。要是我們用你的矛，刺你自己的盾，那會怎麼樣呢？"大家都大笑起來，賣武器的人連一句話也說不出來了。

Indicate whether the following statements are true or false according to the story.

____ 1) 賣武器的人的矛和盾做得好極了，所以很多人來買。

____ 2) 賣武器的人說他的矛比他的盾好，因為它能刺穿世界上最結實的盾。

____ 3) 雖然這個人的矛和盾是世界上最好的，可是沒有人買。

____ 4) 大家不買他的矛和盾，因為沒人相信(xiāngxìn, believe)他說的話。

____ 5) 要是一個人說話前後不一致 (yízhì, consistent)，就是自相矛盾。

WORDS AND EXPRESSIONS ON SPECIFIC TOPICS
常用量詞 (Commonly Used Measure Words)

包	bāo	pack	一包糖/烟	a pack of sugar/cigarettes
磅	bàng	pound	一磅青菜	a pound of vegetables
杯	bēi	glass/cup	一杯水/茶	a cup/glass of water/tea
本	běn	M for book	一本書/字典/小説	book/dictionary/novel
次*	cì	time (of action)	去了一次/看過一次	went once/seen once
分	fēn	cent; minute	一分錢、一分鐘	a cent/minute
封	fēng	M for letters	一封信	a letter
回*	huí	time (of action)	吃過一回/來了一回	have eaten/come once
斤	jīn	catty (500 grams)	一斤鷄肉/蘋果	a catty of chicken/apples
句	jù	sentence	一句中文	a sentence in Chinese
家	jiā	family/institution	一家人/公司/電影院	family/company/cinema
件	jiàn	item; article	一件事/毛衣/行李	matter/sweater/luggage
棵	kē	M for plants	一棵樹	a tree
塊	kuài	lump, piece, yuan	一塊魚、一塊錢	a piece of fish, one yuan
毛	máo	10 cents	一毛錢	10 cents
瓶	píng	bottle	一瓶水/酒	a bottle of water/wine
片	piàn	slice; stretch	一片面包/樹林	a slice of bread/woods

Lesson 6. The Story of Chinese Idioms   117

WORDS AND EXPRESSIONS ON SPECIFIC TOPICS
常用量詞 (Commonly Used Measure Words) *(continued)*

所	suǒ	M for building	一所房子/學校/醫院	a house/school/hospital
趟*	tàng	M for trip	來/去/走/跑一趟	make a trip to come/go
套	tào	set	一套衣服/家具	a set of clothing/furniture
條	tiáo	long/narrow object	一條魚/蛇/圍巾/路	a fish/snake/scarf/road
碗	wǎn	bowl	一碗飯/湯	a bowl of rice/soup
下*	xià	stroke of action (a little bit)	等/看/考慮/想一下	wait for a minute, have a look, think about
枝	zhī	branch (-shaped)	一枝花/筆/烟	a twig of flowers, a pen/a cigarette
張	zhāng	sheet (things with a flat surface)	一張紙/畫/票/桌子	a sheet of paper, a painting/ticket/table
種	zhǒng	kind, sort	一種人/東西	a kind of people/thing

Note: Words marked with * are measure words for actions.

第七課. 萬里長城

Lesson 7. The Great Wall

Before You Read

Getting Started: Study the picture and answer the questions.

這張畫兒畫的是甚麼?

你聽說過長城嗎?

古代的中國人為甚麼要築長城?

生詞
VOCABULARY

1.	萬	wàn	Nu	ten thousand
2.	里	lǐ	M	a Chinese unit of length (= 1/2 km)
3.	長城	Chángchéng	PN	the Great Wall
4.	長	cháng	SV	long
5.	道	dào	M	measure word for long and slender objects
6.	城牆	chéngqiáng	N	city wall
7.	聞名	wénmíng	SV	famous; well-known
8.	建	jiàn	V	to build; to construct; to establish
9.	為了	wèile	Prep.	for the sake of; in order to
10.	保護	bǎohù	V	to protect
11.	四周	sìzhōu	PW	all around
12.	築	zhù	V	to build; to construct
13.	起	qǐ	Adv.	up
14.	統一	tǒngyī	V/SV	to unify; to unite; unified; united
15.	國家	guójiā	N	country
16.	外國人	wàiguórén	N	foreigner
17.	連接	liánjiē	V	to link; to join
18.	這樣	zhèyàng	IE	in this way
19.	當時	dāngshí	TW	then; at that time
20.	進	jìn	V	to enter; to advance
21.	容易	róngyi	SV	easy
22.	發現	fāxiàn	V	to discover; to find
23.	敵人	dírén	N	enemy

24.	燒火	shāo huǒ	VO	to make a fire; to light a fire
25.	烟	yān	N	smoke
26.	消息	xiāoxi	N	news
27.	傳	chuán	V	to pass on; to convey
28.	電話	diànhuà	N	telephone
29.	電報	diànbào	N	telegraph
30.	種	zhǒng	M	kind; sort; type
31.	辦法	bànfǎ	N	way; means; method
32.	有用	yǒuyòng	SV	useful; effective
33.	女子	nǚzǐ	N	young woman
34.	抓	zhuā	V	to force to go; to arrest
35.	丈夫	zhàngfu	N	husband
36.	窗	chuāng	N	window
37.	衣服	yīfu	N	clothes
38.	當……時	dāng……shí	Conj.	When . . .
39.	找到	zhǎodào	VP	to find
40.	哭	kū	V	to cry; to weep
41.	夜	yè	N	night
42.	倒	dǎo	V	to collapse; to fall
43.	古老	gǔlǎo	SV	ancient
44.	文化	wénhuà	N	culture
45.	象徵	xiàngzhēng	N/V	symbol; to symbolize
46.	親眼	qīnyǎn	Adv.	(to see) with one's own eyes
47.	了不起	liǎobuqǐ	IE	excellent; amazing; remarkable
48.	老話	lǎohuà	N	old saying

49.	扶	fú	V	to support with the hand; to hold by the arm
50.	坐	zuò	V	to sit
51.	休息	xiūxi	V	to rest; to take a break
52.	照相	zhàoxiàng	VO	to take pictures; to photograph
53.	張	zhāng	M	measure word for sheets of paper, pictures
54.	謝謝	xièxie	IE	thank you

Words and Expressions Associated with the Great Wall

秦始皇	Qínshǐhuáng	PN	the first emperor of the Qin dynasty (221–207 B.C.)
烽火臺	fēnghuǒtái	N	beacon tower
孟姜	Mèngjiāng	PN	proper name
不到長城非好漢	bú dào Chángchéng fēi hǎohàn	IE	You are not a real man until you have climbed the Great Wall

First Reading: Getting the Main Ideas

There are two main ideas in this text. The second one is provided. Write down the first main idea after quickly reading the text.

1. _____ 。
2. 孟姜女的故事。

萬里長城

在中國的北方，有一道又高又大的城牆。這就是世界聞名的萬里長城。從東到西，這道城牆有一萬二千多里長。

最早的長城兩千多年以前就開始建了。那時，中國還沒有統一，有很多小國家。這些小國的北邊有些外國人常常來打他們。他們為了保護自己，在國家四周築起了城牆。後來秦始皇統一了中國，就用那些小國的城牆，連接成了這道萬里長城。這樣，當時長城北邊的外國人就打不進中國，中國人也不容易跑到長城外邊去了。

長城上建了很多烽火臺。如果一個烽火臺發現了敵人，就燒起火來。下一個烽火臺上的人看見烟火，也就燒起火來。消息就這樣很快地傳下去了。那時候，人們沒有電話，也沒有電報。所以這種辦法又快又好，非常有用。

雖然長城很有用，可是為了築長城，也死了很多人。有一個故事說，南方有一個叫孟姜的女子，結婚才一天，秦始皇就抓她的丈夫去築長城了。冬天來了，孟姜女看着窗外的大雪，想起在北方的丈夫一定又累又冷，就帶上幾件衣服，去北方看他。她走了幾個月才到了北方。可是當她找到築長城的地方時，才知道她丈夫早就累死了。孟姜非常難過，在丈夫死去的地方一直哭了三天三夜，連長城都哭倒了。

　　現在人們到中國去，都想看看長城。有人說，長城是中國古老文化的象徵；可是也有人說，就是因為有了這道長城，幾千年來中國人看不到外面的世界是甚麼樣子。

Second Reading: Getting the Specific Information

Reread the text and complete the following statements according to the text.

1. 萬里長城在_____。它已經建了_____年了。

2. 中國古時候的小國家築長城是為了_____。

3. 秦始皇_____以後，就用_____連接成了這道萬里長城。

4. 長城築好了以後，_____就不容易來打中國了。

5. 古時候，人們沒有_____，也沒有_____，所以他們用_____來傳送_____的消息。這種辦法又_____又_____。

6. 孟姜女住在中國的_____。

7. 冬天來了，孟姜女帶上幾件衣服，去_____。

8. 孟姜女的故事說明了_____。

9. 現在很多人都去看長城，因為長城是_____的象徵。

10. 也有人說就是因為_____，幾千年來中國人不知道_____。

Understanding the Text Structure

1. Paragraphs divide reading materials into topics. One paragraph is usually about one topic. In this text, there are five paragraphs. Identify the paragraphs in which the following topics can be found.

    a. _____長城是怎麼建起來的。

    b. _____長城象徵甚麼。

    c. _____長城在甚麼地方，有多長。

    d. _____長城有甚麼用。

    e. _____孟姜女的故事。

2. In this lesson, we examine the relationship between the main ideas and their supporting ideas in paragraphs. In the following exercises, the main ideas of each paragraph are listed on the left. Fill in the supporting idea units of the paragraph on the right.

Main Ideas	Supporting Details

Para. 1

在中國的北方，有一道城牆。

name: _____

fame: _____

length: _____

direction: _____

Para. 2

最早的長城

time: _____

cause: _____

effect: _____

result: _____

Para. 3

烽火臺　　　　　　　　　　　　　operation:_____

　　　　　　　　　　　　　　　　　function: _____

　　　　　　　　　　　　　　　　　evaluation: _____

Para. 4

為了築長城，中國死了很多人。　　illustrative example (use a few sentences to write about the story of Mengjiang)

_____

_____

_____

_____

_____

_____

_____

會話
DIALOGUE

(Xiao Wang and Mr. Meng, an elderly overseas Chinese, are on the Great Wall.)

孟：哇！長城這麼高，這麼長啊！我小時候就聽說過秦始皇築長城，孟姜女哭長城的故事。可是還從來沒看見過長城是甚麼樣子。

王：那您這次回中國來，總算可以親眼看看了。

孟：是啊！兩千多年以前的中國人真了不起啊。真不知道他們怎麼能在高山上築起這麼高大的城牆？

王：這麼高的城牆，您走得上來也很了不起啊！中國人有句老話："不到長城非好漢"。那您現在也成了好漢了！

孟：你看！長城上有多少好漢啊！男男女女，老老少少。有走上來的，有跑上來的，誒！那位老太太是她的孫子們扶上來的。

王：孟先生累了嗎？要不要坐下來休息休息？

孟：不休息了。我要再多看一些風景，多照幾張相，帶回美國去給我的朋友們看看。

王：孟先生，您看那兒的風景多好。我給您在那兒照張相吧。

孟：好啊！我站在這兒怎麼樣？

王：您再走過去一點，對了，很好。一，二，三，好了。

孟：謝謝！今天我玩得真高興。謝謝你帶我來看長城！

Practice

1. Ask a classmate about places you should visit in the city/town where your university is situated. Get as much information about these places as possible.

2. Talk with a partner about your favorite place.

語法介紹
GRAMMATICAL POINTS

Directional Complement (DC)

Locomotion verbs such as 上, 下, 進, 出, 回, 過, 起 can be used after another verb as a complement to indicate the direction of the action. They are known as *simple directional complements*. When simple directional complements are combined with the other two locomotion verbs 來/去, they are known as *compound directional complements*. Their combination possibilities are shown below:

Simple DC	來	去	上	下	進	出	回	過	起	到	走
Compound DC			上來	下來	進來	出來	回來	過來	起來	到……來	
			上去	下去	進去	出去	回去	過去		到……去	

Note: 走 can only be a simple DC.
起 can only be combined with 來, but never with 去.

Like resultative complements, directional complements come in two types.

Actual Type of DC

- Verb + simple DC: 拿去, 搬走, 帶來, 築起, 買回, 走進
- Verb + compound DC: 走進來, 跑出去, 燒起來, 傳下去, 買回來

  這本書我看完了, 你拿去給老王吧。
  消息就這樣很快地傳下去了。
  我看見她走進來了。
  我們慢慢地走下去吧。
  你再走過去一點, 站上去一點。
  有走上來的, 有跑上來的, 那位老太太是她的孫子們扶上來的。

- Positions for directional complements and the objects.

  a. Objects come after the simple DC. For example:

  他們在國家四周築起了城牆。
  小王拿走了我的書。

她就<u>帶上</u>幾件衣服，去北方找她的丈夫。

    b. For a compound DC, it is more usual to split the complement, to insert the object (especially when it is a place word) before 來/去. For example:

中國人也不能跑<u>到</u>長城外邊<u>去</u>。

如果一個烽火臺發現了敵人，就燒<u>起</u>火<u>來</u>。

他從書包裏拿<u>出</u>一本書<u>來</u>。

這些<u>照片</u> (zhàopiān, photo)，我要帶<u>回</u>美國<u>去</u>。

Note: Simple directional complements are usually not used in single sentences but more likely used as clauses that provide background information for the main action. Compare the following pair of examples.

我看見她<u>走進來</u>了。

她<u>走進</u>房間，四處看看，沒看見甚麼人，就又走出去了。

Potential Type of DC

Potential directional complements, like resultative complements, can be formed by inserting 得/不 between the verb and the complement, signifying capability and non-capability respectively. For example:

這個東西太重，我一個人搬<u>不</u>出去。

有了長城，外國人就打<u>不</u>進來了。

他的名字你想<u>得</u>起來嗎？

Note 1: The choice-type question of the potential complement consists of an *affirmative form* and a *negative form*. For example:

山這麼高，你的車<u>開得上去開不上去</u>？ (= 你的車開得上去嗎?)

Note 2: Sometimes a modal verb such as 可以 or 能 can be placed before a potential complement to emphasize the possibility/potentiality. For example:

這個東西很輕，我一個人就<u>可以</u>搬<u>得出去</u>。

這個字連我小妹妹也<u>能</u>寫<u>得出來</u>。

句型和詞匯用法
SENTENCE PATTERNS AND WORD USAGE

Study the following examples and create a sentence using each phrase or pattern.

就 vs. 才

1. 最早的長城兩千多年以前就開始建了。
2. 可是當她找到築長城的地方時,才知道他早就累死了。
3. 我要他十點鐘來,他九點鐘就來了。
4. 我要他十點鐘來,他十一點才來。
5. _____。(就)
6. _____。(才)

又……又……

1. 這種辦法又快又好,非常有用。
2. 他們家的新房子又高又大,漂亮極了。
3. 今天天氣不好,又刮風,又下雨。
4. 她又想學英文又想學中文,不知道學甚麼才好。
5. _____。

為了

1. 為了築長城,中國歷史上死了很多人。
2. 為了找到她的丈夫,孟姜女走了很遠的路。
3. 為了孩子們,父母每天工作到很晚。
4. 她每天看中文電視 (diànshì, TV),是為了學好中文。
5. _____。

當時

1. 這樣,當時北方的外國人就打不進中國,中國人也不能跑到長城外邊去。
2. 爸爸二十年前到北京去了,當時我才三歲。

3. 這件事當時我不知道，是別人後來告訴我的。

4. 要是你不想做這件事，當時為甚麼不說出來呢?

5. 我昨天沒告訴你這個消息，因為當時我找不到電話。

6. _____。

當……時

1. 可是當她找到築長城的地方時，才知道他早就累死了。

2. 當我們跑到車站時，車已經開走了。

3. 當他父母聽到這個消息時，難過極了。

4. 當他再一次見到她時，已經認不出她來了。

5. _____。

總算

1. 孟先生早就想來中國看長城，今天總算看到了。

2. 我換 (huàn, change) 了三次車，問了五個人，總算找到了他的家。

3. 你總算回來了! 我們等 (děng, wait) 了你三個鐘頭了!

4. 這個問題我想了很久，現在總算懂了。

5. _____。

從來沒(有) V 過

1. 我還從來沒看見過長城是甚麼樣子。

2. 那條牛從來沒聽過音樂。

3. 雖然我在這個城市住了兩年多了，可是我從來沒去過那個地方。

4. 小王很喜歡喝酒，可是他從來沒有喝過中國酒。

5. _____。

練習
EXERCISES

語音練習 Pronunciation

1. Write the pinyin romanization for the underlined characters.

房子<u>倒</u>了 _____   <u>了</u>不起 _____   睡<u>覺</u> _____   保<u>護</u> _____

北京<u>到</u>了 _____   為<u>了</u> _____   <u>覺</u>得 _____   扶<u>着</u> _____

找<u>到</u> _____   <u>總</u>算 _____   消<u>息</u> _____   <u>烟</u>火 _____

手<u>腳</u> _____   一<u>種</u> _____   <u>燒</u>火 _____   一<u>樣</u> _____

2. Write the characters for the following; pay special attention to the underlined syllables.

xiàng<u>zhēng</u>   <u>dào</u>le   jiàndàlóu

hǎo<u>xiàng</u>   yi<u>dào</u>qiáng kàn<u>jiàn</u>

<u>jiā</u>lǐ   <u>fā</u>xiàn   <u>zhù</u>qǐ

<u>lì</u>shǐ   tóu<u>fà</u>   bāng<u>zhù</u>

漢字練習 Chinese Characters

1. Indicate the radicals of the following characters, and find out their meaning.

   a. 邊 道 連 這 過 迷   (部首: ____, 意思: _____)
   b. 建 庭   (部首: ____, 意思: _____)
   c. 火 燒 烽 烟   (部首: ____, 意思: _____)

2. Using the meaning of the radicals, guess the meaning of the following words. Match the meaning to the characters. (Do not use a dictionary.)

追趕 _____   a. to spread, as creeping plants

熬粥 _____   b. passing by

炎熱 _____   c. to run after

過往 _____   d. to cook congee

烟塵 _____   e. scorching hot

蔓延 _____   f. smoke and dust

3. Which other characters have the same radicals?

   _____

詞匯練習 Vocabulary Practice

1. Rewrite the following sentences with the words provided.

   1) 我是十年前到這兒來的，那個時候，這兒没有這麽多樹。(當時)

   2) 我姐姐做事做得很快，也做得很好。(又……又……)

   3) 張三畫蛇畫得很快，因為他想得到那瓶酒。(為了)

   4) 我想學好中文，所以我要到中國去。(為了)

   5) 我聽到這個消息的時候，難過極了。(當……時)

2. 選詞填空 (Fill in the blanks in the following sentences by selecting appropriate words from the list provided).

   為了   世界聞名   保護   建   發現   辦法   有用   了不起

   1) 世界上的森林 (sēnlín, forest) 越來越少，很多國家都在想辦法_____森林。

   2) 我發現這本書 對學中文很_____。

   3) 我們公司 (gōngsī, company) 想去中國_____一個分公司 (branch of a company)。

   4) 她的這個新發現很_____，在世界上都很有名。

5) 是誰_____了美國？有人說是哥倫布 (Christopher Columbus)，也有人說不是。

6) A：這張畫是誰畫的？

   B：這張畫_____，你不知道是誰畫的嗎？

7) _____做完這個工作，我今天一天都沒有休息。

8) 用烽火臺來傳消息這個_____是誰想出來的？

語法練習 **Grammar**

1. Fill in the blanks with appropriate directional complements according to the context given; use one character per blank.

   e.g., 那時候，消息是怎麼傳__ __的呢？→ 那時候，消息是怎麼傳<u>下</u> <u>去</u>的呢？

1) 姐姐在樓上(lóushàng, upstairs)，她想看書，請你給她拿__ __好嗎？

2) 我的酒怎麼不見了？誰拿___了？

3) 這些書可以在屋子裏頭看，可是不能拿__ __。

4) 弟弟正(zhèng, just)要跑__ __玩兒的時候，爸爸從外頭__ __了。

5) 晚上在外頭可能會有點冷，你最好帶___你的大衣 (dàyī, overcoat)。

6) 這些照片，我們想帶___美國___。

7) 別急，別急，請你坐__ __說。你想___甚麼事來了？

8) A：孟先生說的那本書你買__ __了嗎？在哪兒呢？

   B：買__ __了。在我書包裏頭。

   A：我也想買一本。你可以拿__ __給我看看嗎？

2. Rewrite the following sentences with "verb + potential complement" structure.

   e.g., 這些書不重，我能拿上去。

   → 這些書不重，我<u>拿得上去</u>。

中國人幾千年來沒法子看到外面的世界是個甚麼樣子。
→ 中國人幾千年來<u>看不到</u>外面的世界是個甚麼樣子。

1) 他們說中國話，你能聽懂嗎?

2) 我沒法子買到她要的那種車。

3) 王小姐在外頭說話，你能聽見嗎?

4) 你知道不知道小張到哪兒去了？我們都沒法子找到她。

5) 在中國也能聽到美國音樂嗎?

6) 長城那麼高，那位老太太也能走上去，真是了不起!

7) 這本書，我一天就能看完。

8) 你們學了中文以后，都能找到很好的工作嗎?

9) 長城很高，所以當時北邊的外國人沒法子打進來。

10) 山這麼高，你的車能不能開上去?

綜合練習 **Comprehensive Exercises**

1. Fill in the blanks of the following passage with words provided.

下來　老　少　總算　世界上　回　去　不得了　不
上　　倒　築　親眼　看得見　就　才　出來　又......又......

很多人都知道中國的長城。有人說，中國的長城是_____最長的城牆。他們說，在月亮上看不見地球(dìqiú, the earth)上別的東西，只_____萬里長城。這句話是不是真的，我們不知道，可是這句話說明長城非常高大，也非常長。

我很小的時候，_____聽我媽媽說過孟姜女哭_____長城的故事。可是，直到上了大學，我_____學長城的歷史。我覺得長城的故事很有意思，也覺得孟姜女是一個很好的女人，是很有愛心的人。從那以後，我就一直希望有一天能去中國_____看看長城是甚麼樣子。

兩年以前，我_____到北京去了。一到北京，我就帶_____我的照相機(zhàoxiàngjī, camera)，去看長城。長城築在北京城外的山上，_____高_____大。去看長城的人多得_____。男的女的，_____的_____的，中國人，外國人都有。我在長城上看了很久，也照了不少相，因為我想帶_____美國_____給我的朋友們看。我還想去找孟姜女哭長城的地方，可是找了很久，也找_____到。我問了很多人，大家都說聽說過這個故事，可是誰也說不_____這個地方在哪兒。現在我想，歷史上可能沒有孟姜女這個人。古時候的人傳_____這個故事，是為了告訴我們，_____長城非常難，為了這道長城，中國死了太多的人。

2. Answer the following questions according to the passage above.

1) 很多人相信在月亮上可以看見甚麼？為甚麼？

2) 為甚麼"我"小時候喜歡聽長城的故事？

3) "我"到北京以後做的第一件事是甚麼？為甚麼？

4) 去看長城的是些甚麼樣的人?

5) "我"為甚麼要照那麼多相?

6) "我"想找一個甚麼地方?

7) 為甚麼"我"找不到這個地方?

8) "我"現在相信歷史上真的有孟姜女這個人嗎?

9) 為甚麼古代人要把孟姜女這個故事傳下來?

10) 你覺得中國古時候的人應該不應該築長城?

寫作練習 Writing

1. After reading the story below, summarize it in about ten sentences, starting with "古時候，有一位非常喜歡聽音樂的國王……"

2. Write a short essay about a famous place you have visited, using some of the following expressions.

   古老/了不起/世界聞名/為了/有用/偉大/象徵/又……又……/從來沒 V 過/
   當……時/文化/為了/走過來/開上去/買回來/帶來/照相/休息

閱讀練習 Reading Comprehension

1. Guess the meaning of the following words according to the context.

   | 國王 | guówáng | _____ | 吹竽 | chuī yú | _____ | 樂師 | yuèshī | _____ |
   | 南郭 | Nánguō | _____ | 留 | liú | _____ | 當 | dāng | _____ |

濫竽充數

(濫竽充數: làn yú chōng shǔ, to pass oneself off as one of the players in an ensemble—to be there just to make up the number)

　　很久很久以前，有一位<u>國王</u>。他很喜歡聽音樂，特別喜歡聽<u>吹竽</u>。他有三百位吹竽的<u>樂師</u>。每天這三百位樂師一起給國王吹竽，國王聽得很高興。他給這些樂師很多錢，所以樂師們住得很好，穿得很好，當然，吃得也很好。

有一位叫南郭先生的人，看到國王的樂師們過得那麼好，也想去國王那裏當樂師。雖然他不會吹竽，可是他想："在三百個人裏頭，要是只有我一個人不會吹，沒有人能聽得出來的。"他就去見國王，說他吹竽吹得好極了。國王覺得給他吹竽的人越多越好。就留下了南郭先生。

　　每天，給國王吹竽的時候，南郭先生坐在三百個樂師裏頭，手裏拿着竽，學着別人的樣子，好像也很會吹。一年、兩年、三年過去了，沒有人知道南郭先生一點也不會吹竽。國王給了他很多錢，他的日子過得好極了。

　　後來，老國王死了。他的兒子當了國王。這位年輕的國王也喜歡聽吹竽。可是他不喜歡聽很多人一起吹，所以他叫樂師們一個一個地吹給他聽。南郭先生一看，知道自己再不能"濫竽充數"了，就馬上跑了。

2. 判斷正誤 (Indicate whether the following statements are true or false.)

___ 1) 老國王很喜歡聽吹竽，每天要他的樂師們一個一個地吹給他聽。

___ 2) 因為看到國王的樂師們過得很好，所以南郭先生也想去當樂師。

___ 3) 南郭先生吹竽吹得好極了，所以國王要他留下來了。

___ 4) 南郭先生雖然不會吹竽，可是他天天跟別的樂師學着吹也學會了。

___ 5) 大家都不知道南郭先生只會吹一點兒竽。

___ 6) 年輕的國王跟老國王有一點兒不一樣。

___ 7) 南郭先生不喜歡年輕的國王，所以他就走了。

___ 8) 沒有真本事 (běnshì, ability)，可是混 (hùn, mix) 在有本事的人中間裝 (zhuāng, pretend) 樣子，就叫"濫竽充數"。

WORDS AND EXPRESSIONS ON SPECIFIC TOPICS
旅行 (Travel)

旅行	lǚxíng	travel	票	piào	ticket
旅行社	lǚxíngshè	travel agency	買票	mǎipiào	buy a ticket
旅游	lǚyóu	tour	訂票	dìngpiào	reserve a ticket
導游	dǎoyóu	tour guide	退票	tuìpiào	refund a ticket
飛機	fēijī	plane	售票處	shòupiàochù	ticket office
火車	huǒchē	train	軟座	ruǎnzuò	soft seat
汽車	qìchē	car	硬座	yìngzuò	hard seat
公共汽車	gōnggòng qìchē	bus	軟卧	ruǎnwò	soft sleeper
地鐵	dìtiě	subway	硬卧	yìngwò	hard sleeper
出租車	chūzūchē	cab, taxi	單程	dānchéng	one way
司機	sījī	driver	來回	láihuí	round trip
船	chuán	ship/boat	幾點開	jǐdiǎnkāi	When does it depart?
自行車	zìxíngchē	bike	幾點到	jǐdiǎndào	When does it arrive?
單車	dānchē	bike	站臺	zhàntái	platform
坐飛機	zuòfēijī	take a plane	地圖	dìtú	map
開車	kāichē	drive (a car)	上車	shàngchē	aboard; get on
租車	zūchē	rent a car	下車	xiàchē	get off
飛機場	fēijīchǎng	airport	旅館	lǚguǎn	hotel
車站	chēzhàn	station	單人房	dānrénfáng	single room
碼頭	mǎtou	pier	雙人房	shuāngrénfáng	double room

WORDS AND EXPRESSIONS ON SPECIFIC TOPICS
旅行 (Travel) *(continued)*

行李	xíngli	luggage	套房	tàofáng	suite
寄存處	jìcúnchù	luggage room	廁所	cèsuǒ	toilet/restroom
長途	chángtú	long distance	衛生間	wèishēngjiān	bathroom
隨身行李	suíshēn xíngli	carry on luggage	洗手間	xǐshǒujiān	washroom

第八課. 李白學習的故事

Lesson 8. Li Bai Learns a Lesson

Before You Read

Getting Started: Study the picture and discuss it.

1. 圖中的老人在做甚麼？
2. 他們在說甚麼？

生詞
VOCABULARY

1.	學習	xuéxí	V	to study; to learn
2.	歷史	lìshǐ	N	history
3.	詩	shī	N	poetry; verse
4.	詩人	shīren	N	poet
5.	唐朝	Tángcháo	PN	Tang Dynasty
6.	一直	yìzhí	Adv.	always; all along
7.	讀	dú	V	to read (aloud)
8.	翻譯	fānyì	V/N	to translate; translation
9.	外語	wàiyǔ	N	foreign language
10.	外國人	wàiguórén	N	foreigner
11.	努力	nǔlì	V/SV/N	to make great efforts; to try hard; effort
12.	記性	jìxing	N	memory
13.	下工夫	xiàgōngfu	VO	to put in time and energy
14.	容易	róngyì	SV	easy
15.	驕傲	jiāoào	SV	arrogant; proud
16.	刻苦	kèkǔ	SV	hardworking; painstaking
17.	根	gēn	M	measure word
18.	鐵	tiě	N	iron
19.	棒	bàng	N	stick; club
20.	石頭	shítou	N	stone; rock
21.	磨	mó	V	to grind
22.	奇怪	qíguài	SV	strange; surprising; odd
23.	幹	gàn	V	to do

#	漢字	Pinyin	POS	Meaning
24.	針	zhēn	N	needle
25.	敢	gǎn	MV	to dare
26.	相信	xiāngxìn	V	to believe in; to have faith in
27.	耳朵	ěrduo	N	ear
28.	粗	cū	SV	wide (in diameter); thick
29.	越來越......	yuèláiyuè	Adv.	more and more
30.	細	xì	SV	thin; slender
31.	總	zǒng	Adv.	sooner or later; eventually
32.	把	bǎ	Prep.	grammatical particle
33.	感動	gǎndòng	V/SV	to move; to touch; touching
34.	知識	zhīshi	N	knowledge
35.	進步	jìnbù	N/V	to progress; to improve; progress; improvement
36.	終於	zhōngyú	Adv.	at last; finally
37.	成	chéng	V	to become
38.	深	shēn	SV	deep
39.	成為	chéngwéi	V	to become
40.	教育	jiàoyù	V/N	to educate; education
41.	恆心	héngxīn	N	perseverance (in)
42.	忘了	wàngle	V	to forget
43.	剛才	gāngcái	Adv.	just now; a moment ago
44.	農夫	nóngfū	N	peasant; farmer
45.	凍	dòng	V	to freeze
46.	救活	jiùhuó	VP	to save (a life)
47.	可憐	kělián	SV	pitiful; to take pity on
48.	胸口	xiōngkǒu	N	chest

49. 暖和	nuǎnhuo	SV	warm
50. 感激	gǎnjī	V	to feel grateful; indebted
51. 咬	yǎo	V	to bite; to snap at
52. 天性	tiānxìng	N	natural instincts; nature
53. 坏人	huàirén	N	evildoer; scoundrel

First Reading: Getting the Main Ideas

There are two main ideas in the text. The first one is provided. Read the text and fill in the second one.

1. 李白看老太太磨針的故事。

2. _____。

李白學習的故事

李白是中國歷史上最有名的大詩人。他生活在唐朝。從古代到現在，中國人一直都很喜歡讀李白的詩。人們把李白的詩翻譯成很多種外語，很多外國人也喜歡讀他的詩。

李白小時候非常聰明，可是他學習不太努力。他相信自己記性好，平時不用下很多功夫就能很快地學會要學的東西。對他來說，學習是一件很容易的事。因為李白學東西學得快，他就有些驕傲，讀書也不夠刻苦，上課的時候常常跑出去玩，他的老師很為他着急。

有一天，李白又在上課的時候到一條小河邊去玩。他看到一位老太太，手裏拿着一根鐵棒，在河邊的一塊大石頭上磨。李白覺得很奇怪，就走過去問她："老奶奶，您在幹甚麼呢？"老太太說："我要用這根鐵棒磨一根針。"李白不敢相信自己的耳朵。他又問："這麼粗的鐵棒怎麼能磨成一根小小的針呢？"老太太告訴他："只要我每天磨，鐵棒就會越來越細。總有一天我會把它磨成針的。"

李白聽了老太太的話，非常感動。他想：這位老太太這麼老了，還每天努力，想把一根鐵棒磨成一根針。我這麼小，要是不努力學習，長大以後，怎麼能做一個有知識、有用的人呢？

從這一天起，李白就開始努力學習，天天進步。他讀了很多很多書，學到了很多知識，終於成了最有名的詩人。後來，人們就用這個"只要功夫深，鐵棒磨成針"的故事來教育孩子們好好讀書。

Li Bai (701–762) Li Bai was one of the greatest poets in Chinese history. A major poet in the Tang Dynasty, Li Bai was a romantic who wrote about the joys of nature, love, friendship, solitude, and wine. His most famous poems include "Thoughts in Night Quiet" (床前明月光), "Beneath the Moon: Drinking Alone" (花間一壺酒), "Long Time Thinking of You" (長相思，在長安) and "Ching-ping Tunes" (雲想衣裳花想容).

　　Li Bai was born in 701 in Sichuan province. He began to live as a wanderer at the age of nineteen. In his lifetime, he traveled to most parts of the country and enlarged the scope of his poetry. In 742 he arrived at the Tang capital of Chang'an and lived for a time among the other poets at court without ever getting an official appointment. Li Bai was a wanderer all his life. In 757 he joined an expedition, led by one of the emperor's sons, to put down a rebellion in southern China. Accused of trying to set up an autonomous kingdom, the prince was arrested and executed. Li Bai was jailed for a time and then released. He died in 762 in Anhui province.

Second Reading: Getting the Specific Information

Reread the text and indicate whether the following statements are true or false. Write "T" for true and "F" for false.

_____1. 李白小時候學習很努力，所以後來成了有名的詩人。

_____2. 李白剛開始的時候不太明白老太太要用鐵棒做甚麽。

_____3. 那個老奶奶相信鐵棒能磨成針。

_____4. 李白不相信老奶奶能把鐵棒磨成針，因為老奶奶太老了。

_____5. 李白從小就想要做一個有知識，有名的人。

_____6. 只有聰明人才會寫詩。

_____7. 李白幫助老奶奶把鐵棒磨成了針。

Understanding the Text Structure

Identify the important information in the story according to the categories of a "story structure."

1. Characters:

   1). Name of the protagonist _____

   2). Traits of the protagonist and the second person.

   a. _____

   b. _____

2. Setting: _____

Lesson 8. Li Bai Learns a Lesson   151

3. Plot outline:

   1). Event _____

   _____

   _____

   2). Attempt: _____

   _____

   3). Consequence: How did the story end? _____

   _____

   4). What is the moral of the story? _____

   _____

會話
DIALOGUES

(一)

(After class, Xiao Wang and Xiao Zhang are discussing the text they just learned.)

王：你喜歡看甚麼書？

張：我非常喜歡念詩。

王：你想長大以後成為詩人嗎？

張：是啊！如果一個人努力學習，就會成為詩人嗎？

王：我想會的。

張：可是，我昨天很努力，一晚上都没睡覺，怎麼寫不出詩來呢？

王：只努力一個晚上怎麼够呢？

張：那麼我應該怎麼做呢？

王：你應該天天努力，做事情要有恆心。另外你還要先把中文學好，多看一些書，多讀一些詩才能慢慢學着寫詩。

張：對不起，我要去上課了。一直在談寫詩，差一點把上課的事忘了。

王：好吧，晚上再見。我希望你總有一天能學會寫詩。

(二)

張：小李，你剛才看的是甚麼書？

李：是農夫和蛇的故事。

張：農夫和蛇的故事？聽起來好像很有意思。你能不能給我說說？

李：好吧。書上說，在一個很冷很冷的冬天，有一個農夫在路上看到了一條蛇，那條蛇快要凍死了。農夫把蛇拿起來，想救活它。

張：噢？這個農夫喜歡蛇嗎？

李：他不喜歡蛇。可是看到這條蛇快要凍死了，他很可憐它，就把這條蛇拿起來，放到了自己的胸口上。

張：最後農夫把蛇救活了嗎？

李：救活了。這個農夫的胸口很暖和，蛇慢慢地活過來了。

張：那麼這條蛇一定會很感激這個農夫，對不對？

李：你說錯了。它一醒來就咬了這個農夫一口，把他咬死了。

張：天哪！它為甚麼把救它的人咬死了呢？

李：咬人是蛇的天性啊。你救了它的命，它也會咬你。

張：這個農夫真可憐。他真不該救這條蛇。

李：對。這個故事就是要告訴人們，不要可憐蛇，也不要幫壞人的忙。

Practice: Talk about the topics below with your classmates.

1. 一個人是聰明重要還是努力重要？你覺得李白的故事有意義嗎？為甚麼？
2. 介紹一些李白的短詩。
3. 你聽說過別的有名的人學習的故事嗎？能不能給我們講一個這樣的故事？

語法介紹
GRAMMATICAL POINTS

Sentence Pattern Using 把

This pattern is unique to the Chinese language and is difficult for English speakers to learn because it uses a structure that is not common in English.

When and Why a Speaker Uses the 把 Construction

The primary purpose is to focus on one particular thing/matter and to stress the effects of an action upon its object. The second consideration is that when the 把 construction is used, the object must be definite (i.e., it was mentioned previously or could be inferred from context). Under these conditions 把 is particularly appropriate for giving instructions.

The basic pattern of the 把 construction:

S	(Adv.)	把	Object (definite)	V+ complement	
他	沒	把	鐵棒	磨	成針
老奶奶	終於	把	那條蛇	救	活了
請你		把	這本書	放	在那兒

When using the 把 pattern, two things are necessary.

A. The object appearing in this pattern must be "definite" rather than "indefinite." In other words, the noun phrase representing the object must be "the noun" rather than "a noun."

   1. 我要把這本書看完。   I want to finish reading this book.

   2. 我要把一本書看完。   I want to finish reading a book.

Although the second English sentence is correct, the Chinese sentence is not, because of the indefinite nature of the object, "a book."

B. The verb phrase in the 把 pattern must include the result of the action.

Verb + resultative complement

   1. 你應該先把中文學好。   You should first learn Chinese well.

2. 李老師把這件事說清楚了。   Teacher Li has <u>explained</u> this matter <u>clearly</u>.

Verb + directional complement
   1. 小王把書<u>扔出去了</u>。   Xiao Wang threw the book <u>out</u>.
   2. 請把電腦<u>放在桌子上</u>。   Please <u>put</u> the computer <u>on the table</u>.

Verb + 了
   1. 老太太把他的名字<u>忘了</u>。   The old lady <u>forgot</u> his name.
   2. 他把我的蘋果<u>吃了</u>。   He <u>ate</u> my apple.

Compare:
   1. 把這張桌子搬出去。   Please move the table out. (" out" is the result)
   2. *請把這張桌子搬。   Please move the table.

Even though the English version of sentence 2 is correct, the Chinese sentence is not grammatical because the verb phrase does not include a result.

句型和詞匯用法
SENTENCE PATTERNS AND WORD USAGE

Study the following examples and create a sentence using each phrase or pattern.

把A V 成B

This pattern implies that A has become B as the result of an action. The construction following the verb must be a noun phrase.

1. 他想把一根鐵棒磨成一根針。
2. 他把"我"寫成"找"了。
3. 我把李老師看成高老師了。
4. _____。

只要……就…… (so long as; provided that)

1. 只要我每天磨，鐵棒就會越來越細。
2. 你只要做完功課，就可以走了。
3. 只要我在，你就不用着急。
4. 只要你努力學習，就會成為有知識的人。
5. _____。

……，終於…… (at last; in the end; finally)

1. 他讀了很多書，終於成了最有名的詩人。
2. 錢先生想了很久，終於想出了一個辦法。
3. 我寫了一個星期，終於把那首詩寫完了。
4. 他多次想說，但是終於沒有說出口。
5. _____。

多V…… (V more …)

1. 你要多看一些書，多讀一些詩才能慢慢學着寫詩。
2. 我媽媽說多喝水對身體好。

3. 昨天晚上他很累，所以多睡了一個小時的覺。

4. _____。

努力

1. 李白小時候很聰明，可是學習不太努力。

2. 只有努力學習，長大以後才能成為一個有知識有用的人。

3. 他家爸爸媽媽努力工作，孩子們都努力學習。

4. _____。

越來越……

1. 老太太只要每天磨，鐵棒就會越來越細。

2. 天氣越來越冷了。

3. 最近幾年，去中國學漢語的美國人越來越多。

4. _____。

感動

1. 李白聽了老太太的話很感動。

2. 看了這本書，我感動得睡不着覺。

3. 這是一個非常感動人的故事。

4. _____。

練習
EXERCISES

語音練習 Pronunciation

1. Write the pinyin romanization for the underlined characters.

<u>着</u>急	<u>不</u>努力	<u>磨</u>成針	一<u>根</u>
拿<u>着</u>	<u>不</u>太努力	怎<u>麼</u>	一<u>塊</u>
<u>粗</u>	很<u>深</u>	相<u>信</u>	因<u>為</u>
<u>出</u>去	出<u>生</u>	高<u>興</u>	成<u>為</u>

2. Write the characters for the following; pay special attention to the underlined syllables.

cō<u>ng</u>ming	<u>b</u>ùguǎn	zuìj<u>ìn</u>
yǒu<u>m</u>íng	jìn<u>bù</u>	<u>jìn</u>lái
gǎn<u>d</u>òng	<u>jiào</u>yù	ěr<u>duo</u>
bù<u>g</u>ǎn	<u>zhào</u>gù	<u>duō</u>shǎo

漢字練習 Chinese Characters

1. Write the meaning of the following radicals.

心(忄) _____

金 _____

耳 _____

2. From the meaning of the radicals, guess the meaning of the following words. Match the meaning to the words. Do not use a dictionary.

釘錘 _____   a. exercises patience (mentally)

聆教 _____   b. hear of; be told

忍耐 _____   c. clock

鐘 _____   d. hear your words of wisdom

聽說 _____   e. meditate on the past; reflect on an ancient event

懷古 _____   f. claw hammer; nail hammer

詞匯語法練習 Vocabulary and Grammar

1. Fill in the blanks with words provided.

相信　有名　聰明　奇怪　感動　進步　有用　著急　開始
只要……就……　粗　細

1) "這麼粗的鐵棒怎麼能磨成針呢？"李白覺得很_____。

2) 小時候不努力學習，長大以後怎麼能做一個_____的人呢？

3) 鐵棒磨針的故事_____了李白。

4) _____的時候，李白不_____鐵棒可以磨成針。

5) 李白學習的故事告訴我們：_____努力_____一定可以_____。

6) 這個故事很_____，人人都知道。

7) 我真為那個老太太_____，她甚麼時候才能把鐵棒磨成針？

8) "我覺得那個老太太真不_____，她不應該用那麼_____的鐵棒，她應該用一根_____一點的"。

2. Fill in the blanks with words provided.

看　變　長　念

1) 幾年不見，他已經_____成大人了。

2) 真對不起，你跟你哥哥長得太像了，我把你_____成他了。

3) 真不敢相信，以前那個天天玩兒，不學習的孩子現在_____成一個大詩人了。

4) 他把"老太太"_____成"老大大"了。

3. Translate the following sentences into Chinese (using the 把 structure).

1) Please take him to the front of the house.

2) Put the computer over there. (放, to put)

3) You should finish reading that book tomorrow.

4) He threw away the book I gave him.

5) Yi shot down nine suns from the sky.

6) He has finished painting the picture.

7) He ate my food!

綜合練習 **Comprehensive Exercises**

Fill in the blanks with appropriate words.

　　張明是一個很_____的詩人，很多人都喜歡念他的詩。他小_____，母親常常_____他念詩，他每次聽了都非常_____。張明最喜歡_____李白的詩。后來慢慢長大了，他_____開始學習寫詩。可是他_____寫不好，所以常常_____這件事着急。張明想："我_____聰明，為甚麼寫不好詩呢？"他去問母親，母親說："你雖然很聰明，_____知識太少，要_____看書。"張明聽了母親的話，_____天天看書，努力學習怎麼_____詩寫好。後來他的_____越來越多，他的詩也_____好，他終於_____了一個很有名的詩人。

寫作練習 Writing

Write an essay called 難忘的一件事 about a memorable thing that happened to you in your childhood. Use some of the following expressions in your essay.

成為/壞人/教育/外語/知識/感激/只要……就……/越來越……/努力/容易/記性/終於

閱讀練習 Reading Comprehension

Helpful Vocabulary

座	zuò	a measure word	方便 fāngbiàn	convenient
搬	bān	to move	挖 wā	to dig; excavate
運	yùn	carry; transport	神仙 shénxiān	immortal

Read the story quickly and then circle the correct answer to complete the following sentence.

這個故事主要說的是：

1) 一個老人挖山感動了上帝的故事。
2) 老人想叫他的兒子和孫子挖山的故事。
3) 一個老人的家門前有大山，他一家人出門不方便。

　　很久很久以前，有一個老人。他家前面有兩座大山。一家人出門很不方便。這個老人想把這兩座大山搬走，就每天帶著兒子孫子去挖山，把挖下來的土運到東海去。

　　有一位朋友看到他們天天挖山，覺得很奇怪，就對老人說："你們這樣做真是太笨了。這兩座山那麼高，你們幾個人怎麼能挖得完呢？"老人說："我挖不完有我兒子，我兒子挖不完還有我孫子，孫子還會有兒子孫子。這兩座山雖然很高，可是不會再長高了，挖一點就會少一點，總有一天我們會把它們挖完的。"老人不聽那個朋友的話，還是天天帶著全家人努力挖山。

　　這件事終於感動了上帝。他就叫兩個神仙把那兩座山搬走了。

回答問題：

1. 老人為甚麼要挖這兩座大山？

2. 老人的朋友為甚麼覺得老人挖山很奇怪？

3. 這兩座山這麼高，老人想他怎樣才能把它們挖走？

4. 最後這兩座山是怎麼搬走的？為甚麼？

5. 你覺得這個老人的辦法怎麼樣？

口語練習 **Oral Exercise**

Discussion: What do you think about the story of "老人挖山"？

WORDS AND EXPRESSIONS ON SPECIFIC TOPICS
校園生活 (Campus Life)

1.	大學	dàxué	university
2.	學院	xuéyuàn	college; institute
3.	系	xì	department
4.	校園	xiàoyuán	campus
5.	教室	jiàoshì	classroom
6.	開學	kāixué	school opening
7.	放假	fàng jià	vacation
	放(春/暑/寒)假	fàng(chūn/shǔ/hán) jià	spring break/summer vacation/winter break
8.	辦公室	bàngōngshì	office
9.	老師	lǎoshī	teacher
10.	圖書館	túshūguǎn	library
11.	借書	jièshū	to borrow books
12.	還書	huánshū	to return books
13.	閱覽室	yuèlǎnshì	reading room
14.	課	kè	class; course
15.	選課	xuǎnkè	to choose classes; to take classes
16.	上課	shàngkè	to attend class; to start class
17.	下課	xiàkè	to dismiss class
18.	請假	qǐng jià	on leave
	請(病/事)假	qǐng(bìng/shì) jià	leave of absence (because of illness, etc.)
19.	成績	chéngjī	score; result; grade
20.	學分	xuéfēn	credit; point

WORDS AND EXPRESSIONS ON SPECIFIC TOPICS
校園生活 (Campus Life) *(continued)*

21.	作業	zuòyè	homework
22.	練習	liànxí	exercise
23.	考試	kǎoshì	examination; test
	期中/末考試	qīzhōng/qīmò kǎoshì	midterm/final exam
24.	聽寫	tīngxiě	dictation
25.	測驗	cèyàn	test
26.	主修	zhǔxiū	major
27.	專業	zhuānyè	specialty
28.	餐廳	cāntīng	cafeteria

第九課. 神農和中藥

Lesson 9. Shen Nong and Chinese Medicine

Before You Read

Getting Started: Study the pictures and discuss them.

1. 你能看出來圖中的東西是藥嗎?
2. 這種藥跟你常吃的藥有甚麼不一樣?

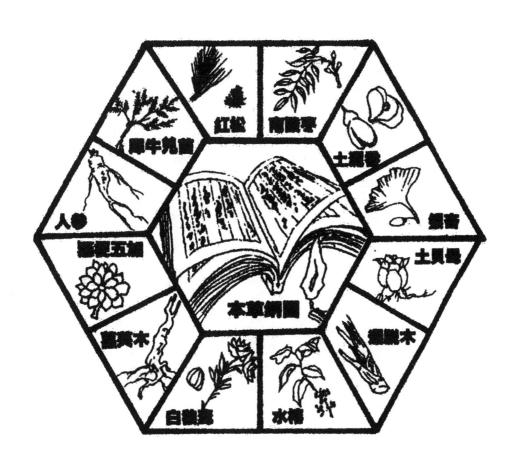

生詞
VOCABULARY

1.	中藥	zhōngyào	N	Chinese herbal medicine
2.	得	dé	V	to get; to obtain
3.	病	bìng	N	disease
4.	得	děi	MV	to have to; must
5.	西藥	xīyào	N	Western medicine
6.	看上去	kànshàngqù	VP	to look; to seem; to appear
7.	草根	cǎogēn	N	grass roots; roots of an herb
8.	樹葉	shùyè	N	leaf
9.	水果	shuǐguǒ	N	fruit
10.	皮	pí	N	skin
11.	呀	ya	Pt.	soft tone marker
12.	蟲子	chóngzi	N	insect
13.	要是	yàoshì	Conj.	if
14.	也許	yěxǔ	Adv.	perhaps; maybe
15.	治病	zhìbìng	VO	to treat a disease
16.	試	shì	V	to try
17.	求	qiú	V	to beg; to pray for
18.	保佑	bǎoyòu	V	to bless; to protect (by God)
19.	差不多	chàbuduō	SV/Adv.	about, almost
20.	要不然	yàoburán	Conj.	otherwise
21.	等	děng	V	to wait
22.	姜	jiāng	N	family name; ginger
23.	首先……後來	shǒuxiān… hòulái	Adv.	first… then…

24.	教	jiāo	V	to teach
25.	種地	zhòngdì	VO	to farm; to cultivate the land
26.	親自	qīnzì	Adv.	personally; in person
27.	嘗	cháng	V	to taste; to try (food)
28.	毒	dú	N	poison
29.	吐	tù	V	to vomit
30.	瀉(肚子)	xiè (dùzi)	V(O)	to have diarrhea
31.	差一點	chàyìdiǎn	Adv.	almost
32.	大家	dàjiā	N	all of us; everyone
33.	健康	jiànkāng	N/SV	health; healthy
34.	危險	wēixiǎn	N/SV	danger; dangerous
35.	許多	xǔduō	Adv.	many
36.	普通人	pǔtōngrén	N	ordinary people; commoners
37.	感謝	gǎnxiè	V	to thank; to be grateful
38.	活	huó	V	to live
39.	歲	suì	MW	year (of age)
40.	記下來	jìxiàlái	VP	to take down; to record
41.	難吃	nánchī	SV	bad-tasting; distasteful
42.	味道	wèidao	N	taste
43.	有效	yǒuxiào	SV	effective
44.	種	zhǒng	MW	kind; type
45.	果皮	guǒpí	N	fruit skin
46.	小看	xiǎokàn	V	to despise; to look down upon
47.	醫生	yīshēng	N	doctor
48.	剛	gāng	Adv.	moment ago; just

Proper Nouns

神農	Shénnóng	PN	the Chinese agriculture god
孫思邈	Sūn Sīmiǎo	PN	famous Chinese herbalist
李時珍	Lǐ Shízhēn	PN	famous Chinese herbalist

First Reading: Getting the Main Ideas

There are three main ideas in the text. One of them is provided. Read the text to determine the other two. As you read, do not look up all the words in the glossary.

1. 中藥和西藥很不一樣。
2. _____
3. _____

神農和中藥

每個人都會得病，得了病就得吃藥。有的人喜歡吃西藥，有的人喜歡吃中藥。中藥跟西藥很不一樣，看上去都是些草根呀，樹葉呀，水果皮呀，還有很多小蟲子。要是以前沒吃過，你也許不相信中藥能治病。可是，只要試一試，你就會知道，中藥真的不錯。

很久很久以前，中國人不知道甚麼東西可以治病，得了病只能求神保佑，要不然就只能等死。後來，有一個姓姜的人，他首先教人們怎樣種地，人們都叫他神農。以後，他又親自嘗了很多種草根樹葉，看看哪些可以治病，哪些不能治病。好幾次神農吃了有毒的草，又吐又瀉，差一點死了。可是，為了大家的身體健康，他不怕危險，終於找到了許多能治病的草根和樹葉。因為神農為人們做了這麼多好事，普通人感謝他，神也保佑他，他活了差不多一百二十歲。

雖然神農找到了很多種中藥，可是這些藥的名字人們都沒有記下來。後來，又有兩個人試了很多的草根、樹葉。他們把那些能治病的草根、樹葉的名字記下來，寫成了中國最早的藥書。這兩個人一個姓孫，叫孫思邈；一個姓李，叫李時珍。孫思邈和李時珍就成了中國的藥王。

吃過中藥的人都知道，有的中藥很難吃，有的味道還不錯。難吃的藥也許是最有效的藥。中國人常說，要治病就不能怕藥難吃。

Second Reading: Getting the Specific Information

Reread the story and indicate whether the following statements are true or false. Write "T" for true and "F" for false. If a statement is false, correct it.

_____1. 中藥看上去跟西藥一樣。
_____2. 樹葉和小蟲都可以做中藥，草根不行。
_____3. 沒吃過中藥的人也許不相信中藥可以治病。
_____4. 神農是第一個教中國人種地的人。
_____5. 神農試過很多樹葉和草根，所以知道甚麼樹葉和草根可以治病，甚麼不行。
_____6. 神農發現可以治病的草藥以後，就把它們的名字記了下來。
_____7. 李時珍跟神農一樣，試過很多草根和樹葉。
_____8. 中國人把神農跟李時珍叫作"藥王"，因為他們寫了中國的第一本藥書。

Understanding the Text Structure

1. Paragraphs divide a composition into topics of interest. One paragraph is usually about one topic. A key word indicates the topic; the rest of the paragraph provides supportive details for it. Key words are important clues for finding the topic of a paragraph. In the following exercises, key word(s) for each paragraph are listed on the left. Find and write the detailed information on the right.

<u>Key words</u>   <u>Supporting details</u>

Para. 1   中藥   description   _____
                   effectiveness   _____

Para. 2   神農   name   _____

                   first event
                   action   _____
                   consequence   _____

                   second event
                   action
                   experience   _____
                   consequence   _____
                   problem   _____

Para. 3   藥書   names   _____
                   event   _____
                   consequence   _____

2. Summarize the text in one or two sentences.

Lesson 9. Shen Nong and Chinese Medicine   173

會話
DIALOGUE

(Mr. Sun has been absent from class for a few days. When he returns to school, he runs into his friend Mr. Zhang.)

張：小孫，前幾天你怎麼沒來上課啊？

孫：我病了，很不舒服。

張：病了？吃藥了嗎？

孫：吃了好幾種，可是都沒有用。

張：那你為甚麼不試一試中藥呢？

孫：就那些草根、果皮嗎？我從來沒吃過。

張：你不要小看那些草根果皮，它們真的能治病！

孫：我不相信。

張：現在很多美國人都喜歡用中藥了。上一次我病了，吃甚麼藥都沒有用。後來還是一位美國朋友給了我一種叫甚麼根的中藥才治好了我的病。

孫：真的？那我得試一試。

Practice: Write a dialogue about the situation described below.

Situation: You have diarrhea and go to see a doctor.
Setting: Doctor's office
Role play: Team up with one of your classmates, who will play the doctor you visit to ask for some medicine to stop the diarrhea.

Expressions and patterns to use: 不舒服　又吐又瀉　一天兩次
首先……，後來……　　要是……，就……

語法介紹
GRAMMATICAL POINTS

Sequencing in Chinese Narrative Discourse

Sequencing refers to how events and situations are ordered in a sentence. They may be in succession (E_1 before E_2), as simultaneous (E_1 and at the same time E_2) or overlap (during E_1, E_2).

Succession of Events and Situations

The simplest way to arrange events and situations is according to the order in which they occur, without any explicit markers. For example, 我每天晚上都做一樣的事情：吃飯，看書，睡覺。However, this kind of simple sentence is rarely used because in actual communication people use sentences in a certain context. So, Chinese has two kinds of markers to put events in context, the verb-suffix 了 and adverbs of sequence.

Verb-suffix 了

1. 盤古睡醒了，睜開了眼睛看，可是蛋裏頭很黑，看不見東西。
2. 他馬上拿了箭，到最高的山上去，射第一個太陽。
3. 昨天晚上我吃了飯就開始做功課，哪兒都沒去。

Adverbs of Sequence

In most cases, two correlative adverbs are used together to indicate the successive relation between events. In this lesson we saw sentences such as:

1. 有一個姓姜的人，他首先教人們怎樣種地，人們都叫他神農。後來，他又親自嘗了很多草根，樹葉……

首先 and 後來, both movable adverbs, can appear either before or after subjects. When they appear before subjects they are more like conjunctions.
  Some monosyllabic adverbs, such as 先……再…… and 才, which can also indicate sequence, cannot be placed before the sentence's subject.

2. 我先吃飯，再喝湯。
3. 我等他吃完飯才/再去找他。

Simultaneity

Simultaneity is primarily expressed by coordination. In Chinese the most commonly used coordinating words are 一邊……一邊……, 又……又……, and 同時 (tóngshí, at the same time).

1. 她一邊看電視一邊吃飯。

2. 他又說又笑，高興得不得了。

3. 她學中文，同時也學法文。

Overlap

Overlap of E_1 and E_2 is expressed by markers, such as 正(在), 在……的時候, and 在…… 期間 (zài …qījiān, during …).

1. 我正(在)吃飯，突然 (tūrán, suddenly) 聽見有人叫我。

2. 在我吃飯的時候，突然有人叫我。

3. 在北京學習期間，我認識了一位中國老人。

Aspect Marker 過

The aspect marker 過 is used to indicate an experience in the indefinite past, which took place at least once before the time of the utterance.

1. 我去過中國。
   I have been to China.

2. 我沒吃過中藥。
   I've never taken Chinese medicine.

句型和詞匯用法
SENTENCE PATTERNS AND WORD USAGE

Study the following examples and create a sentence using each phrase or pattern.

看上去

1. 小王今天<u>看上去</u>不太舒服。
2. 這種水果<u>看上去</u>很好吃。
3. 那個人<u>看上去</u>不像是中國人。
4. _____。

也許

1. 今天<u>也許</u>會下雨。
2. <u>也許</u>張老師病了，不會來了。
3. 這種藥很難吃，你<u>也許</u>不喜歡，可是醫生説很有效。
4. _____。

要不然

1. 你得吃點兒藥，<u>要不然</u>，你的病不會好的。
2. 李小姐好像不太想去，<u>要不然</u>我去吧。
3. 我們快走吧，<u>要不然</u>就太晚了!
4. _____。

差一點

1. 昨天我太忙了，<u>差一點</u>忘了女朋友的生日。
2. 不早了，回家吧，<u>差一點</u>就十一點了。
3. 他開車不小心，<u>差一點</u>出了事。
4. _____。

練習
EXERCISES

語音漢字練習 Pronunciation and Characters

1. Write the pinyin romanization for the underlined characters.

種地	得到	吃藥	神農
一種	一定得去	一次	醫生
治病	蟲子	水果	草根
親自	從前	幾歲	差一點

2. Write the characters for the following; pay special attention to the underlined syllables.

wèidao	chángyicháng	jiànkāng
yīnwèi	chángchang	kànjiàn
shìyishì	zhōngyào	shǒuxiān
yàoshì	yàoburán	shuǐjiǎo

3. Write the meaning of the following radicals.

竹 _____
礻 _____
疒 _____
艹 _____

4. From the meaning of the radicals, guess the meaning of the following words. Match the meaning to the word. (Do not use a dictionary.)

祀 _____   a. seed mat
痛 _____   b. ancestral temple

肄業_____ c. sacrifice to the gods or ancestors

蘆席_____ d. ache; pain

癌症_____ e. taro

筆_____ f. to learn, to study (at a certain school)

祠堂_____ g. cancer

芋芳_____ h. pen, writing instrument

4. Write the pinyin romanization for each pair of characters below and practice their pronunciation.

能/冷_____/_____   時/死_____/_____   差/擦_____/_____

吃/次_____/_____   種/總_____/_____   書/蘇_____/_____

治/字_____/_____   神/森_____/_____

語法詞匯練習 Grammar and Vocabulary

1. 請用"了"或"過"填空 (Fill the blanks with 了 or 過).

   1) A. 你吃_____中藥嗎?

      B. 我常吃。今天剛吃_____一些。

   2) A. 聽說你病_____,現在好_____嗎?

      B. 我以前得_____這種病,知道該吃什麽藥,已經好多_____。

   3) A. 你常常說要去中國玩兒,已經去_____ _____嗎?

      B. 還沒去呢。學好_____中文就去。

2. Rearrange the following events according to the order in which they may occur without using explicit sequential markers.

   他媽媽叫他試試中藥   他去看病   看看那些草根、樹葉

   他吃了三種西藥都沒有用   小張昨天不舒服   他不敢吃

   小張從來沒吃過中藥   醫生叫他吃藥

3. Fill in the blanks in the following paragraph with expressions indicating the timing of events. Expressions may be used more than once.

後來， 在……的同時， 在……的時候， 了， 就， 才， 一邊……一邊

_____ 人們還不會種地 _____，他們只能吃樹上的果子，或者吃打死的動物。_____ 有一個姓姜的人教會 _____ 人們種地，人們 _____ 開始自己生產糧食。_____ 教人們種地 _____，這個姓姜的人還找到 _____ 很多草藥。他常常 _____ 種地 _____ 找藥，許多地裏的草 _____ 都成 _____ 藥。

口語練習 Oral Exercises

1. Share your opinion with your classmates about medicine in general and Chinese herbal medicine in particular.

3. Discussion: Which is better? Chinese herbal medicine or Western conventional medicine? (中藥和西藥哪個好)?

寫作練習 Writing

After reading the story below, state your opinion about medical treatment in an essay called 生病和吃藥. Be sure to support your opinion with examples.

閱讀練習 Reading Comprehension

Helpful Vocabulary

從來	cónglái	always	醫生	yīshēng	doctor
鐵	tiě	iron	醫院	yīyuàn	hospital
力氣	lìqi	strength	承認	chéngrèn	admit
休息	xiūxi	rest	關係	guānxì	matter; relation

2. Read the following passage quickly and answer the following questions.

1) 老孫喜歡吃藥嗎?

2) 為甚麼"鐵人"死了?

"鐵人"

老孫今年四十三歲，又高又大，身體好極了。他能吃能睡，從來不生病。大家都說老孫是個"鐵人"。

有一天早上老孫覺得很不舒服，沒有力氣，也不想吃東西。他太太說："今天不要去上班了，在家好好休息休息吧。"可是老孫想："我是鐵人，怎麼能生病呢？"所以他還是去上班了。第二天老孫更不舒服了，吃的早飯都吐了出來。他太太說，"你今天不能再去上班了，找醫生看看吧。"可是老孫說他沒有病，他不想去醫院。

老孫的太太知道老孫一定不會承認自己生病了，所以她就說："好，就算你沒有病，可是你不舒服，吃一點中藥吧。大家都知道，中藥這東西，有病的人吃了能治病，沒病的人吃了也沒關係，因為有的中藥對身體很好。"老孫說："我不吃藥，我的身體已經夠好了。"

到了第三天，老孫已經病得不能吃也不能喝了。他太太馬上把他送到醫院去，醫生給他吃了很多藥，可是都沒有用。過了兩天，老孫就死了。

3. Indicate whether the following statements are true (T) or false (F) according to the story.

____1) 老孫能吃能睡，身體很好。

____2) 老孫不舒服的時候常常找醫生看病。

____3) 很多中藥對身體有好處，不生病的人也可以吃。

____4) 老孫常常吃中藥，所以身體很好。

____5) 後來老孫病了，病得不能吃不能喝，醫生給他吃的藥太多，他就死了。

WORDS AND EXPRESSIONS ON SPECIFIC TOPICS
問路 (Asking for Directions)

到……怎麼走?	Dào ……zěnme zǒu?	How can I get to…?
去……坐幾路車?	Qù ……zuò jǐ lù chē?	Which bus should I take to go to…?
離這兒有多遠?	Lí zhèr yǒu duōyuǎn?	How far is it from here?
要不要換車?	Yàobúyào huànchē?	Do I have to change?
能坐地鐵去嗎?	Néng zuò dìtiě qù ma?	Can I get there by subway?
坐出租車得多少錢?	Zuò chūzūchē děi duōshǎo qián?	How much does it cost to take a taxi?
走路得多長時間?	Zǒulù děi duōcháng shíjiān?	How long does it take to walk there?
汽車(地鐵)站在哪兒?	Qìchē(dìtiě)zhàn zài nǎr?	Where is the bus (subway) station?
一直往前走嗎?	Yìzhí wǎng qián zǒu ma?	Should I go straight ahead?
要過幾個路口?	Yào guò jǐ gè lùkǒu?	How many intersections do I have to cross?
得用過街天橋嗎?	Děi yòng guòjiētiānqiáo ma?	Do I have to use the overpass?
往左拐還是往右拐?	Wǎng zuǒ guǎi háishì wǎng yòu guǎi?	Should I turn left or right?
就在附近嗎?	Jiùzài fùjìn ma?	Is it nearby?
在路左還是路右?	Zài lùzuǒ háishì lùyòu?	Is it on the left-hand side or on the right-hand side?

第十課. 中國菜

Lesson 10. Chinese Food

Before You Read

Getting Started: Study the pictures and discuss them.

1. 你喜歡吃中國菜嗎?
2. 做中國菜應該用甚麼調料?

生詞
VOCABULARY

1.	氣候	qìhòu	N	climate; weather
2.	飲食	yǐnshí	N	food and drink; diet
3.	習慣	xíguàn	N/V	custom; habit; to become accustomed to
4.	主食	zhǔshí	N	staple food; principal food
5.	溫和	wēnhé	SV	mild, moderate
6.	季	jì	N	season of the year
7.	新鮮	xīnxiān	SV	fresh; new
8.	品種	pǐnzhǒng	N	breed, variety
9.	主要	zhǔyào	SV	main; major
10.	等	děng	N	etc.
11.	比較	bǐjiào	Adv./V	relatively; to compare
12.	各	gè	Pron.	each; every
13.	特點	tèdiǎn	N	characteristic; distinguishing feature
14.	總的來說	zǒngdeláishuō	IE	generally speaking
15.	甜	tián	SV	sweet
16.	鹹	xián	SV	salty
17.	辣	là	SV	hot; peppery; spicy
18.	或者	huòzhě	Conj.	either ... or ... (in affirmative sentence)
19.	酸	suān	SV	sour; tart
20.	講究	jiǎngjiu	SV/V	to be particular about; to stress; to strive for
21.	切	qiē	V	to cut; to slice

22. 形狀	xíngzhuàng	N	shape; form
23. 方法	fāngfǎ	N	method; way; means
24. 重要	zhòngyào	SV	important
25. 請客	qǐngkè	VO	to entertain guests; to give a dinner party
26. 不但……而且	búdàn…érqiě	Conj.	not only…but also
27. 準備	zhǔnbèi	V/N	to prepare; to get ready; preparation
28. 不管……都	bùguǎn…dōu	Conj.	no matter; regardless of
29. 聞	wén	V	to smell
30. 民族	mínzú	N	ethnic group; nationality
31. 雖然……但是	suīrán…dànshi	Conj.	although; though
32. 筷子	kuàizi	N	chopsticks
33. 重視	zhòngshì	V	to pay attention to; to take something seriously
34. 座位	zuòwèi	N	seat; place
35. 叫做	jiàozuò	V	to be called; to be known as
36. 上座	shàngzuò	N	the seat for the guest of honor
37. 按照	ànzhào	Prep.	according to
38. 傳統	chuántǒng	N	tradition
39. 主人	zhǔrén	N	host
40. 讓	ràng	V	to give away; to yield; to allow
41. 客人	kèrén	N	guest
42. 不但……也	búdàn…yě	Conj.	not only…but also
43. 飯館	fànguǎn	N	restaurant
44. 人民	rénmín	N	the people
45. 美味	měiwèi	N	delicious food; delicacy

46. 伯伯	bóbo	N		uncle; one's father's elder brother; also used as affectionate term of respect for an elder
47. 廚師	chúshī	N		cook; chef
48. 空	kòng	N		free time; spare time
49. 聊	liáo	V		to chat
50. 星期	xīngqī	N		week
51. 禮物	lǐwù	N		gift; present

Proper Nouns

四川	Sìchuān	a province in China
湖南	Húnán	a province in China
山西	Shānxī	a province in China
山東	Shāndōng	a province in China
麥當勞	Màidāngláo	McDonald's

Words in This Lesson Relating to Food

<u>蔬菜</u>	<u>shūcài</u>	<u>vegetable</u>
白菜	báicài	Chinese cabbage
土豆	tǔdòu	potato
蘿卜	luóbo	turnip; radish
<u>調料</u>	<u>tiáoliào</u>	<u>condiment; seasoning</u>

糖	táng	sugar
鹽	yán	salt
醋	cù	vinegar
蔥	cōng	scallion; onion
蒜	suàn	garlic
辣椒	làjiāo	hot pepper; chili
<u>做菜方法</u>	**<u>zuòcàifāngfǎ</u>**	<u>method of cooking</u>
炒	chǎo	stir-fry; fry
蒸	zhēng	steam
炸	zhá	fry in deep fat or oil; deep-fry
煮	zhǔ	boil

First Reading: Getting the Main Ideas

There are three main ideas in the text. The first one and last one are provided. Read the text to determine the second one.

1. 中國南北方的飲食習慣和地方菜的特點。
2. _____
3. 中國菜的<u>影響</u> (influence)。

中國菜

中國地大人多，南北氣候不同，人們的飲食習慣也不同。北方人的主食是麵，南方人的主食是大米。南方氣候溫和，一年四季都有新鮮的蔬菜，所以南方的蔬菜品種比北方多。冬天北方的主要蔬菜有白菜、土豆、蘿蔔等，品種比較少。

中國各地的地方菜都有自己的特點。總的來說，中國的南方人喜歡吃甜的，做菜的時候常常在菜裏放糖；北方人喜歡吃鹹的，做菜的時候常常放很多鹽。四川人和湖南人喜歡吃辣的，做菜的時候常在菜裏放辣椒。山西人喜歡在菜裏放醋；山東人愛吃葱或者蒜。所以人們常說"南甜、北鹹、東辣、西酸"。

中國菜的做法很講究。菜應該切成甚麼樣的形狀，應該用哪種方法做，做多長時間，都很重要。做中國菜常用的方法有炒、蒸、炸、煮等。因為用不同的方法做出來的菜味道不同，所以在家裏請客的時候，中國人不但要準備很多種菜，而且也要用不同的方法去做。但是不管用哪種方法，你做的菜都應該好聞、好吃、好看。

中國有很多民族。雖然每個民族都有自己的飲食習慣，但是很多民族都是用筷子吃飯。另外，中國各民族都比較重視吃飯時的座位，他們把重要的座位叫作"上座"。按照中國的傳統，上座應該給老人或者比較重要的人，所以請人吃飯時，主人應該把上座讓給客人坐。

中國菜的做法很講究，各種地方菜的味道也都有自己的特點，所以中國菜不但中國人愛吃，外國人也愛吃。現在世界上很多國家都有中國飯館。因為常去中國飯館吃飯，很多外國人不但學會了用筷子，而且也學會了自己做中國菜。中國菜已經走出了中國，成了世界人民喜愛的美味。

Second Reading: Getting the Specific Information

Reread the text and indicate whether the following statements are true or false. Write "T" for true and "F" for false. If the statement is false, correct it.

_____1. 南方人的主食跟北方人的不同，因為南方的氣候跟北方的不同。
_____2. 北方人的主食是麵。
_____3. 雖然北方冬天很冷，但是蔬菜的品種很多。
_____4. 在外國的中國飯館沒有筷子。
_____5. 中國西部的菜味道比較甜。
_____6. 在中國，用筷子吃飯的民族很少。
_____7. 中國人在家裏請客的時候，常常做很多種菜。
_____8. 按照中國的傳統，只有客人才可以坐上座。

Understanding the Text Structure

1. Paragraphs divide reading material into topics of interest. One paragraph is usually about one topic. In this lesson, there are five paragraphs. Match the paragraphs with their topic by writing the number of the paragraph on the lines.

   _____ 中國菜的做法。

   _____ 世界上有很多人喜歡中國菜。

   _____ 中國北方人和南方人的飲食習慣。

   _____ 各地方菜的特點。

   _____ 中國各民族吃飯的習慣。

2. Match the specific details below to each main idea in the list.

Main Ideas	Specific Details
a. 南方人和北方人的主食不同。	1. ___ 西部人做菜的時候放很多醋。
b. 南甜、北鹹、東辣、西酸。	2. ___ 北方人常常吃麵。
c. 南方蔬菜品種多。	3. ___ 不同的菜應該用不同的方法做。
d. 中國菜的做法很講究。	4. ___ 南方人愛吃米做的東西。
e. 中國人很重視吃飯時的座位。	5. ___ 南方一年四季都有新鮮的蔬菜。
	6. ___ 請人吃飯時，主人要把上座讓給客人。
	7. ___ 好的中國菜不但要好吃，也要好看。
	8. ___ 北方人做菜常常放很多鹽。

會話
DIALOGUE

(Lao Qian is a retired cook. Xiao Zhang is the son of Mr. Zhang, an old friend of Lao Qian. Today Xiao Zhang has come to visit Lao Qian.)

小張：錢伯伯，聽說您做過很多年廚師。

老錢：你是聽誰說的？

小張：聽我爸說的。

老錢：噢，你爸爸。他怎麼樣？我很久沒看見他了。

小張：我爸很好，他請您有空的時候到他家去坐坐。

老錢：很久沒跟你爸爸聊天了，真應該跟他好好聊聊。

小張：錢伯伯，我今天來找您，是想問您能不能教我做幾個菜。

老錢：哦？你是從甚麼時候開始對做菜有興趣的？

小張：是這樣的：這星期六是我女朋友的生日，她說她不要別的生日禮物，只想吃我做的菜。

老錢：噢……我明白了。你想學做甚麼菜？

小張：我女朋友是四川人，所以我想學做川菜。

老錢：好吧。可是今天我不能教你，今天是我孫子冬冬的七歲生日，他一定要我帶他去麥當勞吃飯。明天怎麼樣？

小張：明天幾點？

老錢：下午四點怎麼樣？

小張：四點很好！謝謝您，錢伯伯！

老錢：不用謝，明天見！

Practice: Prepare a dialogue about the situation described below.

You don't know how to do Taiji and want to learn it from Master Li, your friend Xiao Li's father. Today you run into Master Li and ask him if he can teach you Taiji.

語法介紹
GRAMMATICAL POINTS

The 是......的 Construction

The 是......的 construction is used to highlight the circumstances related to an event or action that *took place in the past*. These circumstances usually include when, where, how, and at whose hands it happened. The 是 in the 是......的 construction is optional unless it is a negative sentence.

The word or phrase indicating the circumstances related to the event is placed immediately after 是 and before the verb, as shown in the following:

Sb./Sth.	(是)	QUESTION/ ANSWER CIRCUMSTANCES	V	的	
王先生	(是)	甚麼時候	到	的	紐約?
他	(是)	十點	到	的。	

1. A: 你是<u>哪年</u>到美國來的?   B: 我是<u>一九八六年</u>來的。
2. A: 小張是<u>從哪兒</u>來的?   B: 聽說他是<u>從上海</u>來的。
3. A: 他是<u>怎麼</u>來的?   B: 他是<u>坐車</u>來的。
4. A: 他是<u>跟誰一起</u>來的?   B: 他<u>跟老李一起</u>來的。
5. A: 今天的晚飯是<u>誰</u>做的?   B: 是<u>老高</u>做的。
6. A: 那本小說是<u>誰</u>寫的?   B: 好像是<u>王老師</u>寫的。

When the O(bject) of the verb is mentioned in the 是......的 construction, it is customary to place the object after the 的. However, if the object is a pronoun it should be placed before 的. Compare the following three sentences.

7. 我們是五年前買的<u>車</u>。
8. 錢伯伯是在我們家吃的<u>晚飯</u>。
9. 你是甚麼時候看見<u>他</u>的?

As mentioned above, the 是......的 construction is used to introduce the circumstances of a past event or action. This requires that the V (O) in the 是......的 construction be a realized action or event. In other words, the 是......的 construction should not be used if the event or action has not taken place (as in example 10). On the other hand, if the speaker knows that the event has already taken place (as in the second and third sets below), the

是……的 construction should be used when circumstances about the event are requested or introduced.

10. A: 小高，你想甚麼時候結婚？　　B: 我明年五月結婚。
11. A: 小李，你想甚麼時候結婚？　　B: 我已經<u>結婚了</u>。
　　A: 哦？你<u>是</u>甚麼時候結<u>的</u>婚？　　B: 去年五月。
12. A: 你<u>是</u>甚麼時候買<u>的</u>這本書？　　B: 我<u>是</u>去年買<u>的</u>。
　　A: 你<u>是</u>在哪兒買<u>的</u>？　　B: 我<u>是</u>在中國買<u>的</u>。
　　A: 這本書<u>是</u>誰寫<u>的</u>？　　B: <u>是</u>王老師寫<u>的</u>。
　　A: <u>是</u>王老師在哪兒寫<u>的</u>？　　B: 對不起，我不知道。

The negative form of the 是……的 construction is 不是……的. For example:

13. 他們<u>不是</u>今天早上到<u>的</u>，是昨天早上到的。
14. 我們<u>不是</u>在這家飯館吃<u>的</u>魚。
15. 那<u>不是</u>我寫<u>的</u>。是他替我寫的。

句型和詞匯用法
SENTENCE PATTERNS AND WORD USAGE

Study the following examples and create a sentence using each phrase or pattern.

不管……都……

1. 不管用哪種方法做，你做的菜都要好聞、好吃、好看。
2. 不管明天下不下雨，我們都要去。
3. 這個孩子很不聽話。不管父母說甚麼，他都不聽。
4. _____。

講究

1. 中國菜的做法很講究。
2. 他不講究穿，但是很講究吃。
3. 去年小李結婚的時候，買了很多非常講究的衣服。
4. _____。

按照

1. 按照中國的傳統，上座應該給老人或者比較重要的人。
2. 這個菜，你應該按照錢伯伯教你的方法做。
3. 按照王先生的說法，北京的冬天比較冷。
4. _____。

準備

1. 在家裏請客的時候，中國人常常會準備很多種菜。
2. 你應該早一點兒作準備，現在準備太晚了。
3. 你們把結婚的東西都準備好了嗎?
4. _____。

總的來說

1. 在中國，各地的地方菜都有自己的特點。總的來說，中國的南方人喜歡吃甜的，做菜的時候常常在菜裏放糖；北方人喜歡吃鹹的，做菜的時候常常放很多鹽。
2. 我在這兒工作五年了。總的來說，這個工作不太忙，比較舒服。
3. 雖然這本書有些小問題，但是總的來說寫得不錯。
4. _____。

或者 vs. 還是

1. 今天晚飯你想吃白菜還是吃魚？
2. 白菜或者魚都可以。
3. 王先生的中文好還是李先生的中文好？
4. 你今天去或者明天去沒有甚麼不同。
5. _____。

練習
EXERCISES

語音練習 Pronunciation

1. Write the pinyin romanization for the underlined characters.

   廚師 -- 出生　　　講究 -- 長江　　　蔬菜 -- 樹葉　　　新鮮 -- 相信

   很粗 -- 喝醋　　　飲食 – 意思　　　酸味 -- 葱蒜　　　鹽水 -- 眼睛

2. Write the characters for the following; pay special attention to the underlined syllables.

jiàozuò	rénmín	kuàizi
shàngzuò	cōngming	hěnkuài
měiwèi	yǐnshí	qìhòu
yīnwèi	yīnggāi	hòulái

漢字練習 Chinese Characters

1. The characters in each of the following groups share a common radical. Identify the radicals and write the meaning of each radical.

   1)　饅　餃　餓　飽　館

   radical _____　　meaning of radical _____

   2)　粉　粽　糕　梁　糧

   radical _____　　meaning of radical _____

   3)　醒　酸　醋　醉　醬　酒

   radical _____　　meaning of radical _____

2. Write other characters that have the same radicals as the examples above.

_____

詞匯練習 Vocabulary Practice

1. Fill in the blanks with the appropriate word. Each word can be used only once.

各　準備　講究　或者　不同　主食　另外　四季　新鮮　酸

1) 這裏春天很舒服，夏天也不熱，一年_____天氣都很好。
2) 在中國，北方人的_____是麵。
3) 他喜歡住在城外，因為城外的空氣 (kōngqì, air) 很_____。
4) 張伯伯七十歲了。他說生活中的_____甜苦 (kǔ, bitterness) 辣他都嘗過。
5) 他每天吃晚飯都要有六個菜。大家都知道他很_____吃。
6) 我的看法跟你的沒有很大的_____。
7) 我已經把蔥跟蒜都_____好了。
8) 你星期一_____星期二去都可以。
9) 聽說美國_____地都有中國人，是不是真的?
10) 我爸爸每天早上都要喝一點酒。_____，他還要吃兩個土豆，一些水果。

2. Fill in each of the blanks with the appropriate word.

終於　決定　味道　廚師　有名　而且　禮物　雖然　因為　自己　為

　　我昨天去錢伯伯家，請他教我做中國菜。錢伯伯說，他_____教我做兩個菜，一個湯(tāng, soup)。他說這兩菜一湯都是_____的四川菜，_____也都不太難學。昨天下午，我跟錢伯伯學了兩個小時，最後_____把湯跟菜都做好了。

　　_____錢伯伯做過很多年的_____，所以他甚麼菜都會做，而且做得很好。他一邊做一邊給我講，我一邊看一邊跟他學。_____我只學了兩個多小時，可是我覺得學到了不少東西。我們晚上吃的就是我們_____做的這兩菜一湯。晚飯我吃了很多，好吃極了!

今天，我用了兩個小時才把錢伯伯教我的菜和湯做好。不久，我女朋友小李就到了。她看見我_____她做的飯菜，非常高興。她一邊吃一邊說我做的菜_____非常好，而且說這是她得到的最好的生日_____。

語法練習 **Grammar**

1. Asking questions using the 是……的 construction.

    Example: 小王來了。 (when? how?)   a) 她<u>是</u>甚麼時候來<u>的</u>?
                                                                                                         b) 她<u>是</u>怎麼來<u>的</u>?

1) 我昨天買了一本書。   (with how much money?)
2) 他已經吃過早飯了。   (when?)
3) 聽說他們結婚了。   (when? where?)
4) 老李看見張老師了。   (where?)
5) 她父親去過中國。   (how? with whom?)
6) 小林已經學過那個故事了。   (where? with whom?)
7) 我爸爸給了我一本中文小說。 (who wrote the novel?)
8) 小高去年去過中國。   (with whom? how? from where?)
9) 我學過法文。   (how long ago?)
10) "畫蛇添足"我已經學過了。 (when? where?)

2. Complete the following sentences.

1) 雖然這個地方有很多外國學生，_____。
2) 我媽媽做的菜_____，而且非常好看。
3) 不管_____，他都會做。
4) 今天晚上我們應該去吃法國飯，我_____沒吃法國菜了。
5) 老張會說很多種外語。但是總的來說，_____。
6) 我買了一條魚；另外，我_____。

7) 這個菜，請你按照＿＿＿＿＿＿＿＿＿＿＿＿＿＿＿＿＿＿＿＿＿＿＿＿＿＿＿去做。

8) 你說老王彈琴彈得好聽＿＿＿＿＿＿＿＿＿＿＿＿＿＿＿＿小高彈琴彈得好聽?

口語練習 Oral Exercises

1. Discussion: 中國菜和美國菜有甚麼不同?
2. Study the following words and expressions. Make up a dialogue with your classmates.

Helpful Vocabulary

主食

米飯	mǐfàn	(cooked) rice
饅頭	mántou	steamed bun;
麵條	miàntiáo	noodles
餃子	jiǎozi	dumpling

點心

年糕	niángāo	New Year's cake
粽子	zòngzi	pyramid-shaped dumpling made of glutinous rice wrapped in bamboo leaves
元宵	yuánxiāo	sweet dumpling made of glutinous rice flour

蔬菜

菠菜	bōcài	spinach
芹菜	qíncài	celery
芥蘭	jièlán	broccoli
四季豆	sìjìdòu	string bean
茄子	qiézi	eggplant

西紅柿	xīhóngshì	tomato
青椒	qīngjiāo	green pepper
胡蘿蔔	húluóbo	carrot
菜花	càihuā	cauliflower
黃瓜	huángguā	cucumber

肉

雞肉	jī ròu	chicken
牛肉	niú ròu	beef
豬肉	zhū ròu	pork

蛋/奶/豆腐

雞蛋	jīdàn	(chicken) egg
牛奶	niúnǎi	milk
豆腐	dòufu	tofu

海鮮

魚	yú	fish
蝦	xiā	shrimp
龍蝦	lóngxiā	lobster

湯

酸辣湯	suānlà tāng	hot and sour soup
餛飩湯	húntún tāng	wonton soup
蛋花湯	dànhuā tāng	eggdrop soup

水果

蘋果	píngguǒ	apple	桔子	júzi	orange; tangerine
葡萄	pútao	grape	梨	lí	pear
香蕉	xiāngjiāo	banana	草莓	cǎoméi	strawberry

Sample Menu Items

麻婆豆腐	mápó dòufu	Bean Curd with Minced Pork, Sichuan Style
紅燒茄子	hóngshāo qiézi	Stewed Eggplant with Brown Sauce
魚香芥蘭	yúxiāng jièlán	Broccoli with Garlic Sauce
宮保雞丁	gōngbǎo jīdīng	Diced Chicken with Hot Sauce and Peanuts
四季豆牛	sìjìdòu niú	Beef with String Beans
糖醋黃魚	tángcù huángyú	Sweet and Sour Yellow Fish
小籠湯包	xiǎolóng tāngbāo	Steamed Small Meat Dumplings
海鮮炒麵	hǎixiān chǎomiàn	Fried Noodles with Seafood
甜酸肉	tiánsuān ròu	Sweet and Sour Pork
蒜茸菠菜	suànróng bōcài	Spinach with Fresh Garlic
青豆蝦仁	qīngdòu xiārén	Baby Shrimp with Green Peas
清炒黃瓜	qīngchǎo huángguā	Sautéed Cucumber

寫作練習 Writing

Write a short essay, called 飲食和健康, describing the similarities and differences between the eating habits of people in the United States and in China, including your opinion about diet and health. Use some of the following expressions.

是……的/氣候/溫和/特點/總的來說/味道/習慣/蔬菜/不管……都/按照

閱讀練習 Reading Comprehension

Helpful Vocabulary

作家	zuòjiā	writer	將來	jiānglái	future
文章	wénzhāng	article; writings	發財	fācái	make a fortune
立論	lìlùn	present one's argument	官	guān	government official
兆頭	zhàotou	omen	痛打	tòngdǎ	beat soundly

1. Read the following passage quickly and answer the following question after reading:
這個故事主要說的是甚麼？

立論

周伯伯是一位有名的<u>作家</u>，跟我爸爸是多年的好朋友。這幾天我爸爸身體不太好，周伯伯聽說以後，昨天下午就來看他了。他們兩個人天南海北，聊得非常高興。從下午兩點一直聊到媽媽把晚飯做好。媽媽請周伯伯吃了晚飯再走。周伯伯跟我們一起吃完飯以後，我跟弟弟一定要周伯伯給我們講講怎麼才能把<u>文章</u>寫好。周伯伯說："難啊！"然後他就給我們講了他小時候的一件事：幾十年以前，當時周伯伯還在上小學。一天，他在上課的時候準備作文，問老師<u>立論</u>的方法。"難！"老師看著周伯伯的眼睛回答："我告訴你一件事：一家人生了一個男孩，父母高興極了。孩子一個月的時候，父母為了得到一點好<u>兆頭</u>，就把孩子抱出來給客人們看。

一個客人說：'這孩子<u>將來</u>要<u>發財</u>的。'他也得到一些感謝。

一個客人說：'這孩子將來要<u>做官</u>的。'他就得到一些好話。

一個客人說：'這孩子將來是要死的。'他得到的是大家的<u>痛打</u>。"

"說要死的人說的是真話，說要發財的人說的是假話。但說假話的得到感謝，說真話的得到痛打。你……"

"我不想說假話，也不想得到痛打，那麼，老師，我應該怎麼說呢？"周伯伯問老師。"那麼，你應該說：'啊呀！這孩子啊！您看！多麼……。哎呀！哈哈！哈哈哈哈！'"

2. 下面的句子說得對不對？Read each of the following statements and decide whether it is true or false according to what you have read above.

_____ 1) 昨天晚上的晚飯是我媽媽做的。

_____ 2) 周伯伯的身體不太好。

_____ 3) 小學老師給周伯伯講這個故事，是想告訴他立論很難。

_____ 4) 因為男孩的父母想得到一些好話，所以才把孩子抱出來給客人看。

_____ 5) 說真話的人得到了孩子父母的感謝；說假話的人得到的是痛打。

_____ 6) 最後老師告訴周伯伯一定要說真話，不要說假話。

3. 回答問題 Answer the following questions.

1) 你覺得哪個客人說得最好？為甚麼？

2) 老師說周伯伯應該怎麼說？你覺得老師的辦法好不好？

WORDS AND EXPRESSIONS ON SPECIFIC TOPICS

買東西 (Shopping)

價格	jiàgé	price
買	mǎi	to buy
賣	mài	to sell
貴	guì	expensive
便宜	piányi	cheap
斤	jīn	*jin* (= 1/2 kilogram)
磅	bàng	pound (unit of weight)
重	zhòng	heavy
輕	qīng	light
多少	duōshǎo	how much; how many
幾	jǐ	how many
市場	shìchǎng	market
超級市場	chāojíshìchǎng	supermarket
商店	shāngdiàn	store
百貨商店	bǎihuòshāngdiàn	department store
書店	shūdiàn	bookstore
藥店	yàodiàn	pharmacy
衣服	yīfu	clothes
褲子	kùzi	pants
肉	ròu	meat
水果	shuǐguǒ	fruit
找錢	zhǎo qián	to give change

Examples:

請問，魚怎麼賣? 　　　　　　先生，您想買點兒甚麼?
請問，魚多少錢一斤? 　　　　這種三塊一斤，那種兩塊五一斤。
請問，魚一斤多少錢? 　　　　先生，找您八塊錢。
請問，這本書多少錢? 　　　　三十六塊。您要幾本?
這種藥一瓶多少錢? 　　　　　一瓶十二塊八。
你們有沒有中文字典? 　　　　對不起，字典賣完了。
肉多少錢一磅?
太貴了，能不能便宜一點兒? 　這個價錢已經很便宜了。
小姐，一共多少錢? 　　　　　一共一百零七塊二。

漢 字 源 流 簡 論

Appendix I
A Brief History of the Creation of Chinese Characters and the Evolution of the Chinese Writing System

The origins of Chinese writing remain obscure. The earliest formative stage of writing appeared in the Neolithic age and was discovered in the twentieth century. These markers are called **Shang-gu-wen-zi** 上古文字 (High Antiquity Figures). Archaeological findings have proved that writing in China started several millennia ago, dating to about 5000 B.C. Most of these markings appear to have been signs used for practical purposes. However, many of these indicative markings and numerals have survived in later writing systems.

Oracle-Bone (甲骨文, carapace and bone) ***Inscription***. The earliest documents we know of, differing only stylistically from the Chinese script of the present, date from the fourteenth century B.C. and lasted to the eleventh century B.C. (from the late Shang to the early Zhou dynasty). These inscriptions were hand-carved on animal bones and tortoise shells and were used to communicate with the supernatural. They are also referred to as divination verses. In the late nineteenth century, oracle-bone inscriptions were identified and immediately accepted as the forebear of the Chinese writing system.

The principles on which the figures, or characters, were formed remain fundamental to the Chinese writing system down to modern times. Each character essentially symbolizes a word, not a sound. This distinguishes the Chinese system from the other great system of the world, the alphabetical system. Each character is fixed; that is, it does not change to indicate gender, number, tense, or grammatical function. Thus the writing system corresponds exactly to the character of the spoken language. When a new word representing something new in the world begins to be used, a new character is devised.

From about the age of the oracle-bone inscriptions, the script evolved into several new styles.

The Great-Seal Script style 大篆 was derived from both pictorial and oracle-bone inscriptions. This script became more abstract. The size, columns, and space began to be regulated. About this time it was realized that written words not only communicated with the divine but could serve mundane purposes.

The Small-Seal Script 小篆 was the national official script designed by the Qin (221-206 B.C.) court. When Emperor Qin Shihuang founded the first empire of China, he also standardized the writing system. The characters in this script type are highly stylized. Each character is confined to a vertically oblong shape. The lines are even, thin, and wiry; the space is carefully regulated, while pictorial elements almost totally disappeared.

The Clerical Script 隸書 developed as state functions multiplied and became more complex. Written records became imperative. In the Qin and Han period (221 B.C. to A.D. 221), the clerical script emerged. It was simplified from seal script for the purpose of clarity in reading and ease of writing. The script reached the height of its popularity in the Later Han period of the second century. At about the same time, the writing tools, notably the writing brush, improved, as a result of which an awareness of aesthetics emerged and calligraphers developed individual modes of expression.

Regular/Standard Script 楷書 developed from the late Han through the fourth and fifth centuries. It is the most commonly used style for printing today.

Draft (Grass) Script 草書 is literally a form of shorthand in which the characters are rendered in dots and short strokes. It originated in the second century B.C. and matured by the third and fourth centuries. Because its abbreviation makes it difficult to read, the draft script is used mainly by scholars. It was recently adopted into simplified Chinese writing used in the People's Republic of China.

Action (Running) Script 行書 is a type that combines the draft and regular scripts. It is easier for the layman to read and is also popular in administrative circles and among artists. It is the most practical style for handwriting in use today.

The Basic Structure of the Chinese Character

Basically there are four types of Chinese characters:

The *pictographic* characters are simplified line drawings of concrete objects. Examples are ⊙ sun 日, ☽ moon 月, 馬 horse 馬, and 龜 tortoise 龜. Even without any help or hint, we can see the meaning through the picture the ancient Chinese provides here. Although the writing forms have changed, we still can find a trace of their origins.

Ideographic characters are graphic representations of abstract ideas; that is, for ideas that do not have a physical form that can be readily rendered into a line drawing format, an abstract symbolic representation is created. Examples are: "above" 上, "below" 下, and 凶 "evil" or "malevolent." Since the concept of "above" and "below" are always comparative, it was very difficult to express them, and the ancient people tried to use a dot or shorter line placed either above or below the horizontal boundary line to indicate the concepts of "above" ⟂ "below" ⊤. The character 凶 "malevalent" represents a deep pit ⌣ into which an unwary traveler has fallen. The ✕ indicates danger and the feeling of fear and surprise at the unexpected fall.

Compound-Ideographic Characters combine two or more character elements into a new compound character; for example, when a "person" 人 is tired, he naturally seeks out a "tree" 木 where he can take a short break, so these two components combine to form the character meaning "to rest" 休. A thing that is "large" 大 at the bottom and gradually becomes "small" 小 at the top is pointed, so the character for "small" and "large" combine to form the character "pointed" or "sharp" 尖.

Radical-Phonetic Compounds combine a "radical" with a phonetic element. This method is the most popular way of forming Chinese characters. For example, 酒 "wine" or "alcohol" has a phonetic element "container" 酉 and a radical element "water or liquid" 氵. Another example is "to take a wife or to marry a woman" 娶. The phonetic element "to take" indicates the pronunciation of the character; the other part, "woman" 女, has the functional meaning of a female as wife. In the character "sleep" 睡, the phonetic element is "to hand down" or "to fall down" and the element that carries the meaning is "eye" 目. Together, it means when a person's "eyes fall down," he sleeps.

Hailong Wang

詞彙表

APPENDIX II
Comprehensive Vocabulary List
(English – Chinese)

Definition/ function	Character	Pinyin	Part of speech	Lesson no.
about, almost	差不多	chàbuduō	SV/Adv.	9
a little	一點兒	yìdiǎnr	IE	6
a respectful address term for elderly men	老大爺	lǎodàye	N	6
according to	按照	ànzhào	Prep.	10
adverbial marker	地	de	Pt.	5
after, later	以後	yǐhòu	TW/Adv.	2
again	又	yòu	Adv.	5
all	都	dōu	Adv.	1
all around	四周	sìzhōu	PW	7
all of us; everyone	大家	dàjiā	N	9
almost	差一點	chàyìdiǎn	Adv.	9
already	已經	yǐjing	Adv.	2
although, though	雖然	suīrán	Adv.	6
although; though	雖然……但是	suīrán … dànshi	Conj.	10
altogether	一共	yígòng	Adv.	2
America	美國	měiguó	PN	1
ancient	古	gǔ	SV	4
ancient	古老	gǔlǎo	SV	7
and	和	hé	Conj.	2
animal	動物	dòngwu	N	1
arrogant; proud	驕傲	jiāoào	SV	8
arrow	箭	jiàn	N	4
as if; seemingly	好像	hǎoxiàng	Adv.	6
at; on; in	在	zài	CV	2

* not required to be memorized

Definition/function	Character	Pinyin	Part of speech	Lesson no.
autumn	秋	qiū	N	1
away from	離	lí	CV	6
back; behind; rear	後面	hòumian	L/PW	1
bad-tasting; distasteful	難吃	nánchī	SV	9
beautiful; pretty; abbreviation for America	美	měi	SV/N	1
because; because of; due to	因為	yīnwèi	Conj.	3
become	成為	chéngwéi	V	8
before; formerly; previously	以前	yǐqián	TW/Adv.	1
behind	後頭	hòutou	L/PW	3
Beijing (Peking)	北京	Běijīng	PN	1
big	大	dà	SV	2
birthday	生日	shēngrì	N	2
black; dark	黑	hēi	SV	5
blood	血	xiě, xuè	N	5
blossom; abbreviation for England	英	yīng	N	1
body	身體	shēntǐ	N	5
book	書	shū	N	3
both sides	兩邊	liǎngbiān	PW	3
bottle	瓶	píng	N/M	6
breath; air; gas	氣	qì	N	5
breed, variety	品種	pǐnzhǒng	N	10
bright; brilliant	明	míng	SV	1
brothers	兄弟	xiōngdì	N	2
busy	忙	máng	SV	2
can, to be able to	能	néng	MV	2
capital	首都	shǒudū	N	3
certain; certainly; definitely	一定	yídìng	SV/Adv.	1
characteristic; distinguishing feature	特點	tèdiǎn	N	10
chariot; (horse-drawn) carriage	馬車	mǎchē	N	6
child	孩	hái	N	1

Definition/function	Character	Pinyin	Part of speech	Lesson no.
China	中國	zhōngguó	PN	1
Chinese cabbage	白菜	báicài	N	10
Chinese god of agriculture	神農	Shénnóng	N	9
Chinese herbal medicine	中藥	zhōngyào	N	9
Chinese unit of length (= 1/2 km)	里	lǐ	M	7
chopsticks	筷子	kuàizi	N	10
city	城市	chéngshì	N	3
city wall	城牆	chéngqiáng	N	7
clean	乾淨	gānjìng	SV	5
climate; weather	氣候	qìhòu	N	10
clothes	衣服	yīfu	N	7
cloud	雲	yún	N	5
cold	冷	lěng	SV	3
comfortable	舒服	shūfu	SV	4
commonly used	常用	cháng yòng	SV	1
completely; entirely; absolutely	完全	wánquán	Adv.	4
condiment; seasoning	*調料	tiáoliào	N	10
cook; chef	廚師	chúshī	N	10
country	國家	guójiā	N	7
culture	文化	wénhuà	N	7
custom; habit	習慣	xíguàn	N	10
danger; dangerous	危險	wēixiǎn	N/SV	9
dare	敢	gǎn	MV	8
deep	深	shēn	SV	8
delicious food; delicacy	美味	měiwèi	N	10
doctor	醫生	yīshēng	N	9
draw; paint/drawing, painting	畫	huà	V/N	6
each; every	各	gè	Pron.	10
ear	耳朵	ěrduo	N	8
east	東	dōng	N.	3
easy	容易	róngyi	SV	7

Definition/function	Character	Pinyin	Part of speech	Lesson no.
effective	有效	yǒuxiào	SV	9
egg	蛋	dàn	N	5
eight	八	bā	Nu.	2
either . . . or . . . (in affirmative sentence); or	或者	huòzhě	Conj.	10
enemy	敵人	dírén	N	7
English	英文	yīngwén	N	2
enough	夠	gòu	SV/Adv.	6
even . . .	連...都...	lián...dōu...	IE	6
evening	晚上	wǎnshang	N	4
every	每	měi	Pron.	4
evildoer; scoundrel	壞人	huàirén	N	8
excellent; amazing; remarkable	了不起	liǎobuqǐ	IE	7
expressing complaint or impatience	哎呀	āiyā	interj.	6
extremely	極了	jíle	IE	6
extremely; terribly; awfully	不得了	bùdéliǎo	IE	6
extremely; unusually; extraordinarily	非常	fēicháng	Adv.	4
eye	眼睛	yǎnjīng	N	5
family	家庭	jiātíng	N	2
family name; ginger	姜	jiāng	N	9
famous Chinese herbalist	*李時珍	Lǐ Shízhēn	PN	9
famous Chinese herbalist	*孫思邈	Sūn Sīmiǎo	PN	9
famous; well-known	聞名	wénmíng	SV	7
far; distant	遠	yuǎn	SV	6
fast; quick	快	kuài	SV	6
father	爸爸	bàba	N	2
father	父	fù	N	1
female (as modifier only)	女	nǚ	SV	1
few	少	shǎo	SV	2
finally; at last	總算	zǒngsuàn	Adv.	4
finally; the last	最後	zuìhòu	Adv.	4

Definition/function	Character	Pinyin	Part of speech	Lesson no.
first . . . then . . .	首先……後來	shǒuxiān...hòulái	conj.	3
fish	魚	yú	N	3
five	五	wǔ	Nu.	2
flour	麵	miàn	N	3
flower; abbreviation for China	*華	huá	N	1
follow-up question marker	呢	ne	Pt.	1
food and drink; diet	飲食	yǐnshí	N	10
foot	腳	jiǎo	N	5
foot	足	zú	N	6
for	為	wèi	CV	2
for (for the benefit of); to; to give	給	gěi	CV/V	2
for (take the place of); to replace	替	tì	CV/V	2
for example	比方說	bǐfāngshuō	IE	1
for the sake of; in order to	為了	wèile	Prep.	7
foreign language	外語	wàiyǔ	N	8
foreigner	外國人	wàiguórén	N	7
four	四	sì	Nu.	2
free time; spare time	空	kòng	N	10
fresh; new	新鮮	xīnxiān	SV	10
friend	朋友	péngyou	N	2
from	從	cóng	Prep.	3
fruit	水果	shuǐguǒ	N	9
fruit skin	果皮	guǒpí	N	9
garlic	*蒜	suàn	N	10
general measure word	個	gè	M	1
generally speaking	總的來說	zǒngdeláishuō	IE	10
generation	代	dài	M	2
gentleman; Mr.; husband	先生	xiānsheng	N	1
gift; present	禮物	lǐwù	N	10
given name; full name	名字	míngzi	N	1
god; spiritual being	神	shén	N	4

Definition/function	Character	Pinyin	Part of speech	Lesson no.
good; benefit; advantage	好處	hǎochù	N	6
good; well	好	hǎo	SV	1
Good-bye	再見	zàijiàn	IE	1
grammatical particle	把	bǎ	Prep.	8
grandfather	爺爺	yéye	N	2
grandmother	奶奶	nǎinai	N	8
grass roots; roots of an herb	草根	cǎogēn	N	9
great	*偉	wěi	SV	1
great; mighty	偉大	wěidà	SV	7
guest	客人	kèrén	N	10
hair	頭髮	tóufa	N	5
happy; glad	高興	gāoxìng	SV	1
hardworking; painstaking	刻苦	kèkǔ	SV	8
have to; must	得	děi	MV	9
head/measure word for animals	頭	tóu	N/M	6
health; healthy	健康	jiànkāng	N/SV	9
heavy	重	zhòng	SV	5
here	這兒	zhèr	PW	2
Hey!	欸	éi	Interj.	6
high, tall	高	gāo	SV	3
history	歷史	lìshǐ	N	8
horse; a surname	馬	mǎ	N	1
host	主人	zhǔrén	N	10
hot	熱	rè	SV	3
hot pepper; chili	*辣椒	làjiāo	N	10
hot; peppery; spicy	辣	là	SV	10
house	房子	fángzi	N	3
How are things? How about...?	怎麼樣	zěnmeyàng	IE	5
human being; person; people	人	rén	N	1
hundred	百	bǎi	Nu.	1
hundred million	*億	yì	Nu.	2

Definition/function	Character	Pinyin	Part of speech	Lesson no.
husband	丈夫	zhàngfu	N	7
I am sorry; Excuse me	對不起	duìbuqǐ	IE	1
I; me	我	wǒ	Pron.	1
idea	主意	zhǔyi	N	2
idiom; set phrase	成語	chéngyǔ	N	6
if	要是	yàoshì	Conj.	9
if; in case	如果	rúguǒ	Conj.	4
immediately	馬上	mǎshàng	Adv.	4
important	重要	zhòngyào	SV	10
in addition; besides	另外	lìngwài	Conj.	10
in the front	前頭	qiántou	L/PW	3
in this way	這樣	zhèyàng	IE	7
in; inside	裏	lǐ	Loc.	2
indicates a change of state	了	le	Pt.	2
insect	蟲子	chóngzi	N	9
intelligent; bright	聰明	cōngming	SV	5
interest	興趣	xìngqu	N	6
interesting	有意思	yǒuyìsi	SV	4
iron	鐵	tiě	N	8
it	它	tā	Pron.	6
It doesn't matter; Never mind	沒關係	méiguānxi	IE	1
It doesn't matter; Never mind.	不要緊	búyàojǐn	IE	6
just now; a moment ago	剛才	gāngcái	TW	8
kind; sort; type	種	zhǒng	N/M	7
knowledge	知識	zhīshi	N	8
lady; Mrs.; wife	太太	tàitai	N	1
lake	湖	hú	N	3
leaf	樹葉	shùyè	N	9
left	左	zuǒ	N/Lco.	3
light	輕	qīng	SV	5
long	長	cháng	SV	7

Definition/function	Character	Pinyin	Part of speech	Lesson no.
long (time)	久	jiǔ	SV	5
love/to love/love	愛	ài	MV/V/N	3
low; to lower	低	dī	SV/V	3
main; major	主要	zhǔyào	SV	10
male (as modifier only)	男	nán	SV	1
many	許多	xǔduō	Adv.	9
many; much	多	duō	SV	1
marker (of noun modifier)	的	de	Pt.	1
matter; event; thing; business	事情	shìqing	N	4
May I ask	請問	qǐngwèn	IP	1
may; can	可以	kěyǐ	MV	2
McDonald's restaurant	*麥當勞	Màidāngláo	PN	10
meaning	意思	yìsi	N	1
measure word for clothes or matters	件	jiàn	M	2
measure word for long and slender object	根	gēn	M	8
measure word for long and slender objects	道	dào	M	7
measure word for tree, etc.	棵	kē	M	3
memory	記性	jìxìng	N	8
method; way; means	方法	fāngfǎ	N	10
middle	中間	zhōngjiān	PW	3
mild, moderate	溫和	wēnhé	SV	10
Miss; young lady	小姐	xiǎojie	N	1
modern times; modern	現代	xiàndài	N/SV	2
moment ago; just	剛	gāng	Adv.	9
money	錢	qián	N	2
moon	月亮	yuèliang	N	5
more and more	越來越	yuèláiyuè	Adv.	8
most (used to form superlative)	最	zuì	Adv.	3
mother	媽媽	māma	N	2
mother	母	mǔ	N	1

Definition/function	Character	Pinyin	Part of speech	Lesson no.
mountain	山	shān	N	3
mouth; MW for member of a family	口	kǒu	N/M	2
muddled; confused; bewildered	糊塗	hútu	SV	6
music	音樂	yīnyuè	N	6
musician	音樂家	yīnyuèjiā	N	6
mutually, each other	互相	hùxiāng	Adv.	2
MW for river and long, narrow things	條	tiáo	M	3
name; given name	名	míng	N	1
namely; to be no other than	就是	jiùshì	adv./VP	4
narrow	窄	zhǎi	SV	3
nationality; ethnic group	民族	mínzú	N	10
natural instincts; nature	天性	tiānxìng	N	8
necessary; necessity	必要	bìyào	SV/N	6
needle	針	zhēn	N	8
new	新	xīn	SV	5
news	消息	xiāoxi	N	7
night	夜	yè	N	7
nine	九	jiǔ	Nu.	2
no matter; regardless of	不管…都…	bùguǎn…dōu	Conj.	10
no; not	不	bù	Adv.	1
north	北	běi	N	3
not only...but also...	不但…而且…	búdàn…érqiě	Conj.	10
now; at present	現在	xiànzài	TW	2
of course	當然	dāngrán	Adv.	6
often	常常	chángcháng	Adv.	2
Oh!	噢	ō, ò	Interj.	1
okay	行	xíng	SV	5
old	老	lǎo	SV	2
old saying	老話	lǎohuà	N	7
older brother	哥哥	gēge	N	2

Definition/function	Character	Pinyin	Part of speech	Lesson no.
older sister	姐姐	jiějie	N	2
on the ground; on the earth	地上	dìshang	N	4
one	一	yī	Nu	1
one of the Warring States (770–256 B.C.)	楚國	Chǔguó	PN	6
one's surname is; surname	姓	xìng	V/N	1
only	只	zhǐ	Adv.	2
ordinal number prefix	第	dì	Prefix	4
ordinary people; commoners	普通人	pǔtōngrén	N	9
origin; source	來源	láiyuán	N	1
originally; essentially	本來	běnlái	Adv.	6
other people	別人	biérén	Pron.	6
other; alternative	別的	biéde	Pron.	5
otherwise	要不然	yàoburán	Conj.	9
outside	外	wài	Loc.	3
ox; cow; bull; a surname	牛	niú	N	1
part, section	部	bù	Loc.	3
Particle	啊	a	Pt.	2
particle	嘛	ma	Pt.	2
pattern	樣	yàng	N	2
peasant; farmer	農夫	nóngfū	N	8
perhaps; maybe	也許	yěxǔ	Adv.	9
perseverance in)	恆心	héngxīn	N.	8
personally; in person	親自	qīnzì	Adv.	9
physical strength; effort	力氣	lìqi	N	4
chest	胸口	xiōngkǒu	N	8
pitiful	可憐	kělián	SV	8
place name	地名	dìmíng	N	1
place; space	地方	dìfang	N	1
please; to invite	請	qǐng	V	1
poet	詩人	shīrén	N	8

Definition/function	Character	Pinyin	Part of speech	Lesson no.
poetry; verse	詩	shī	N	8
poison	毒	dú	N	9
polite measure word for persons	位	wèi	M	1
potato	*土豆	tǔdòu	N	10
pretty good	不錯	búcuò	SV	5
pretty; good-looking	好看	hǎokàn	SV	3
probably; maybe; possible	可能	kě'néng	Adv./SV	1
problem; question	問題	wèntí	N	2
a province in China	*湖南	Húnán	PN	10
a province in China	*山西	Shānxī	PN	10
a province in China	*四川	Sìchuān	PN	10
a province of China	*山東	Shāndōng	PN	10
recent	最近	zuìjìn	TW	5
relatively; compare	比較	bǐjiào	Adv./V	10
restaurant	飯館	fàn'guǎn	N	10
rice (uncooked rice)	大米	dàmǐ	N	3
right	對	duì	SV	2
right	右	yòu	N/Loc.	3
river	河	hé	N	3
road	路	lù	N	6
sad; aggrieved	難過	nánguò	SV	4
salt	*鹽	yán	N	10
salty	鹹	xián	SV	10
scallion; onion	*葱	cōng	N	10
season of the year	季	jì	N	10
season of the year	季節	jìjié	N	4
seat for the guest of honor	上座	shàngzuò	N	10
seat; place	座位	zuòwèi	N	10
see	看見	kànjiàn	VP	4
see with one's own eyes	親眼	qīnyǎn	Adv.	7
self	自己	zìjǐ	Pron.	2

Comprehensive Vocabulary List

Definition/function	Character	Pinyin	Part of speech	Lesson no.
separate; to part	分開	fēnkāi	VP	5
seven	七	qī	Nu.	2
several/how many	幾	jǐ	Nu./QW	2
Shanghai City	上海	Shànghǎi	PN	1
shape; form	形狀	xíngzhuàng	N	10
should; ought to	應該	yīnggāi	MV	2
side	邊	biān	N/Loc.	3
side	面	miàn	N/Loc.	3
side	旁邊	pángbiān	PW	3
simply	簡直	jiǎnzhí	Adv.	6
six	六	liù	Nu.	2
skin	皮	pí	N	9
sky; heaven, day	天	tiān	N	4
slow	慢	màn	SV	5
smoke	烟	yān	N	7
snake; serpent	蛇	shé	N	6
so; therefore	所以	suǒyǐ	Conj.	3
soft tone marker	呀	ya	Pt.	9
some	一些	yìxiē	Pron.	2
some	有的	yǒude	Pron.	1
sooner or later; eventually	總	zǒng	Adv.	8
sour; tart	酸	suān	SV	10
south	南	nán	N	3
spring	春	chūn	N	1
staple food; principal food	主食	zhǔshí	N	10
stick; club	棒	bàng	N	8
still, yet	還	hái	Adv.	2
stone; rock	石頭	shítou	N	8
storied building; floor	樓	lóu	N	3
story	故事	gùshì	N.	6
strange; surprising; odd	奇怪	qíguài	SV	8

Definition/function	Character	Pinyin	Part of speech	Lesson no.
stupid	笨	bèn	SV	6
sugar	*糖	táng	N	10
summer	夏天	xiàtiān	N	3
sun	太陽	tàiyáng	N	4
surname	李	Lǐ	N	1
surname	*劉	Liú	N	1
surname	王	Wáng	N	1
surname	張	Zhāng	N	1
surname	*趙	Zhào	N	1
surname	周	Zhōu	N	1
sweat; perspiration	汗	hàn	N	5
sweet	甜	tián	SV	10
symbol; to symbolize	象徵	xiàngzhēng	N/V	7
Tang Dynasty	唐朝	Tángcháo	PN	8
taste	味道	wèidao	N	9
telegraph	電報	diànbào	N	7
telephone	電話	diànhuà	N	7
ten	十	shí	Nu.	2
ten thousand	萬	wàn	Nu	7
that	那	nà/nèi	Pron.	1
the east	東方	dōngfāng	N	4
the front; ahead; preceding	前面	qiánmiàn	L/PW	1
the Great Wall	長城	Chángchéng	PN	7
the head of a family; patriarch	家長	jiāzhǎng	N	2
the more...the more	越……越……	yuè...yuè...	Conj.	6
the name of the god who, according to the legend, created the world	盤古	pángǔ	N	5
the name of the god who, according to the legend, shot down nine suns	羿	Yì	N	4
the north	北方	běifāng	N	3
the people	人民	rénmín	N	10

Definition/function	Character	Pinyin	Part of speech	Lesson no.
the same	一樣	yíyàng	SV	3
the south	南方	nánfāng	N	3
the West	西方	xīfāng	N	4
the world	世界	shìjiè	N	5
then; at that time	當時	dāngshí	TW	7
then; therefore	那麼	name	Conj.	4
there	那裏	nàlǐ	PW	3
there	那兒	nàr	PW	3
these	這些	zhèxiē	Pron.	2
thick	厚	hòu	SV	5
thin; slender	細	xì	SV	8
thing; matter	事	shì	N	2
thing; object	東西	dōngxi	N	2
this	這	zhè/zhèi	Pron.	1
thousand	千	qiān	Nu.	2
three	三	sān	Nu.	2
thunder	雷	léi	N	5
time, moment	時候	shíhou	N	4
time	時間	shíjiān	N	1
tired	累	lèi	SV	3
to add	添	tiān	V	6
to arrive; to reach/to	到	dào	V/CV	4
to ask	問	wèn	V	1
to be	是	shì	V	1
to be born	出生	chūshēng	V	1
to be particular about; to stress; to strive for	講究	jiǎngjiu	SV/V	10
to be standing	站着	zhànzhe	V	5
to become	變得	biànde	VP	4
to become	成了	chéngle	V	8
to become; to change into	變成	biànchéng	VP	5
to beg; to pray for	求	qiú	V	9

Definition/function	Character	Pinyin	Part of speech	Lesson no.
to believe in; to have faith in	相信	xiāngxìn	V	8
to bite; to snap at	咬	yǎo	V	8
to bless; to protect (by God)	保佑	bǎoyòu	V	9
to boil; to cook	*煮	zhǔ	V	10
to break; broken	破	pò	V	5
to bring	帶	dài	V	6
to build; to construct	築	zhù	V	7
to build; to construct; to establish	建	jiàn	V	7
to buy	買	mǎi	V	2
to be called, to be known as	叫做	jiàozuò	V	10
to call; to name; to be named	叫	jiào	V	1
to chat	聊	liáo	V	10
to collapse; to fall	倒	dǎo	V	7
to come out	出來	chūlái	VP	5
to cry; to weep	哭	kū	V	7
to cut; to slice	切	qiē	V	10
to decide; decision	決定	juédìng	V/N	2
to deep fry	*炸	zhá	V	10
to despise; to look down upon	小看	xiǎokàn	V	9
to die	死	sǐ	V	4
to discover; to find	發現	fāxiàn	V	7
to do	幹	gàn	V	8
to do	做	zuò	V	2
to drink	喝	hē	V	6
to drive (a horse or a chariot)	趕	gǎn	V	6
to eat	吃	chī	V	3
to eat (meal); to have meal	吃飯	chīfàn	VO	4
to educate; education	教育	jiàoyù	V/N	8
to enter; to advance	進	jìn	V	7
to entertain guests; to give a dinner party	請客	qǐngkè	VO	10
to farm; to cultivate the land	種地	zhòngdì	VO	9

Definition/function	Character	Pinyin	Part of speech	Lesson no.
to fear; to be afraid	怕	pà	V	4
to feel grateful or indebted	感激	gǎnjī	V	8
to find	找到	zhǎodào	VP	7
to flow	流	liú	V	3
to fly	飛	fēi	V	4
to force to go; to arrest	抓	zhuā	V	7
to forget	忘	wàng	V	8
to freeze	凍	dòng	V	8
to get angry; to take offense; angry; upset	生氣	shēngqì	V/SV	4
to get; to obtain	得	dé	V	9
to get; to obtain; to gain	得到	dédào	V	6
to go; to go to	去	qù	V	4
to grind	磨	mó	V	8
to grow up to look; look	長得	zhǎngde	V	4
to have diarrhea	瀉(肚子)	xiè (dùzi)	V(O)	9
to have not; without	沒有	méiyǒu	V	2
to have; there is/are	有	yǒu	V	1
to heed what an elder or superior says; to be obedient	聽話	tīnghuà	VO/SV	2
to help	幫助	bāngzhù	V	2
to hope; to expect; hope; expectation	希望	xīwàng	V/N	1
to illustrate; to show; to indicate	說明	shuōmíng	V	6
to introduce; introduction	介紹	jièshào	V/N	2
to kick	踢	tī	V	5
to know; to realize; to be aware of	知道	zhīdào	V	4
to know; to recognize; to be acquainted with	認識	rènshi	V	1
to let; to give away; to yield	讓	ràng	V	10
to link; to join	連接	liánjiē	V	7
to live	住	zhù	V	2
to live (one's life)	過日子	guòrìzi	VO	4

Definition/ function	Character	Pinyin	Part of speech	Lesson no.
to live; to be alive	活	huó	V	9
to look after	照顧	zhàogù	V	2
to make a fire; to light a fire	燒火	shāohuǒ	VO	7
to make great efforts; to try hard	努力	nǔlì	V/SV/N	8
to marry	結婚	jiéhūn	VO	2
to move; to touch/ touched; moved	感動	gǎndòng	V/SV	8
to need; to want; to be going to	要	yào	V/MV	2
to open (one's eyes)	睜開	zhēngkāi	VP	5
to pass on; to convey	傳	chuán	V	7
to pass through	經過	jīngguò	V	3
to pass; to spend (time)	過	guò	V	5
to pay attention; to take something seriously	重視	zhòngshì	V	10
to play the zither	彈琴	tánqín	VO	6
to prepare; to get ready; preparation	準備	zhǔnbèi	V/N	10
to progress; to improve	進步	jìnbù	V	8
to protect	保護	bǎohù	V	7
to put; to put in; to add	放	fàng	V	10
to rain	下雨	xiàyǔ	VO	4
to rest; to take a break	休息	xiūxi	V	7
to return; to go back	回	huí	V	4
to rise	上升	shàngshēng	VP	5
to run	跑	pǎo	V	6
to save (a life)	救活	jiùhuó	V	8
to see; to be able to see	見到	jiàndào	V	4
to seem; to appear	看上去	kànshàngqù	VP	9
to sense; to feel	覺得	juéde	V	4
to set up; to establish	設立	shèlì	V	7
to shoot	射	shè	V	4
to sink	下沉	xiàchén	VP	5
to sit	坐	zuò	V	7

Comprehensive Vocabulary List

Definition/function	Character	Pinyin	Part of speech	Lesson no.
to sleep	睡	shuì	V	4
to smell	聞	wén	V	10
to snow	下雪	xiàxuě	VO	3
to speak	說	shuō	V	2
to steam	*蒸	zhēng	V	10
to stir-fry; to fry	*炒	chǎo	V	10
to stop	停	tíng	V	6
to study; to learn	學	xué	V	2
to study; to learn	學習	xuéxí	V/N	8
to support with the hand; to hold by the arm	扶	fú	V	7
to take down; to record	記下來	jìxiàlái	VP	9
to take pictures; to photograph	照相	zhàoxiàng	VO	7
to taste; to try (food)	嘗	cháng	V	9
to teach	教	jiāo	V	9
to thank; to be grateful	感謝	gǎnxiè	V	9
to think; to miss; to want; would like to	想	xiǎng	V/MV	2
to translate; translation	翻譯	fānyì	V/N	8
to treat a disease	治病	zhìbìng	VO	9
to try	試	shì	V	9
to understand; to comprehend	懂	dǒng	V	6
to unify; to unite; unified; united	統一	tǒngyī	V/SV	7
to use; with; by means of	用	yòng	V/CV	2
to vomit	吐	tù	V	9
to wait	等	děng	V	9
to wake up; to be awake	醒	xǐng	V	5
to work; work; job	工作	gōngzuò	V/N	3
together	一塊兒	yíkuàir	Adv.	4
together	一起	yìqǐ	Adv.	2
tomorrow	明天	míngtiān	TW	2
too; also; as well; either	也	yě	Adv.	1

Definition/function	Character	Pinyin	Part of speech	Lesson no.
toward	往	wàng	Prep.	3
toward; to	對	duì	CV	6
tradition	傳統	chuántǒng	N	10
tree	樹	shù	N	3
tree	樹木	shùmù	N	5
tune; melody	曲子	qǔzi	N	6
turnip; radish	*蘿卜	luóbo	N	10
two	二	èr	Nu.	2
two (used before a measure word)	兩	liǎng	Nu.	2
uncle; one's father's elder brother	伯伯	bóbo	N	10
under	下	xià	Loc.	3
unit of currency; piece	塊	kuài	M	2
up	起	qǐ	Adv.	7
urgent; emergent	急	jí	SV	6
useful; effective	有用	yǒuyòng	SV	7
vegetable	*蔬菜	shūcài	N	10
vehicle; car	車	chē	N	6
verb complement marker	得	de	Pt.	6
verb suffix indicating durative state	着	zhe	suffix	5
very; quite	很	hěn	Adv.	1
vinegar	*醋	cù	N	10
voice; sound	聲音	shēngyīn	N	5
warm	暖和	nuǎnhuo	SV	8
way; means; method	辦法	bànfǎ	N	7
weather	天氣	tiānqì	N	4
week	星期	xīngqī	N	10
west	西	xī	N	3
Western medicine	西藥	xīyào	N	9
what	甚麼	shénme	QW	1
when ...	當……時	dāng...shí	Conj.	7
where	哪兒	nǎr	QW	3

Comprehensive Vocabulary List

Definition/function	Character	Pinyin	Part of speech	Lesson no.
who; whom	誰	shéi/shuí	QW	2
why	為甚麼	wèishénme	QW	2
wide	寬	kuān	SV	3
wide (in diameter); thick	粗	cū	SV	8
will; would/ know how to...	會	huì	MV/V	4
wind	風	fēng	N	5
window	窗	chuāng	N	7
wine; alcohol; liquor	酒	jiǔ	N	6
winter	冬天	dōngtiān	N	3
with; and; follow	跟	gēn	CV/V	2
worried; to feel anxious; to worry	着急	zháojí	SV/V	2
Yangtze River	長江	Chángjiāng	PN	3
year (of age)	歲	suì	M	9
yes/no question marker	嗎	ma	Interj.	1
yesterday	昨天	zuótiān	TW	4
you	你	nǐ	Pron.	1
you (respectful, honorific)	您	nín	Pron.	1
young	年輕	niánqīng	SV	6
young	少	shào	SV	2
young woman	女子	nǚzǐ	N	7
younger brother	弟弟	dìdi	N	2
younger sister	妹妹	mèimei	N	2
your (honorific); expensive; costly	貴	guì	SV	1
your honorable surname	*貴姓	guìxìng	IE	1
zero	零	líng	Nu.	2

詞匯表
COMPREHENSIVE VOCABULARY LIST
(CHINESE – ENGLISH)

Pinyin	Character	Part of speech	Definition/function	Lesson no.
a	啊	Pt.	Particle	2
ài	愛	MV/V/N	love/to love/love	3
āiyā	哎呀	interj.	expressing complaint or impatience	6
ànzhào	按照	Prep.	according to	10
ba	吧	Pt.	question marker for presuppositions	1
bā	八	Nu.	eight	2
bǎ	把	Prep.	grammatical particle	8
bàba	爸爸	N	father	2
bǎi	百	Nu.	hundred	1
báicài	白菜	N	Chinese cabbage	10
bànfǎ	辦法	N	way; means; method	7
bàng	棒	N	stick; club	8
bāngzhù	幫助	V	to help	2
bǎohù	保護	V	to protect	7
bǎoyòu	保佑	V	to bless; to protect (by God)	9
běi	北	N	north	3
běifāng	北方	N	the north	3
Běijīng	北京	PN	Beijing (Peking)	1
běnlái	本來	Adv.	originally; essentially	6
bèn	笨	SV	stupid	6
bǐfāngshuō	比方說	IE	for example	1
bǐjiào	比較	Adv./V	relatively; compare	10
bìyào	必要	SV/N	necessary; necessity	6

* not required to be memorized

Pinyin	Character	Part of speech	Definition/function	Lesson no.
biān	邊	N/Loc.	side	3
biànchéng	變成	VP	to become; to change into	5
biànde	變得	VP	to become	4
biéde	別的	Pron.	other; alternative	5
biérén	別人	Pron.	other people	6
bóbo	伯伯	N	uncle; one's father's elder brother	10
búcuò	不錯	SV	pretty good	5
búdàn...érqiě	不但...而且...	Conj.	not only...but also...	10
búyàojǐn	不要緊	IE	It doesn't matter; Never mind.	6
bù	不	Adv.	no; not	1
bù	部	Loc.	part, section	3
bùdéliǎo	不得了	IE	extremely; terribly; awfully	6
bùguǎn...dōu	不管...都...	Conj.	no matter; regardless of	10
cǎogēn	草根	N	grass roots; roots of an herb	9
chàbuduō	差不多	SV/Adv.	about, almost	9
chàyìdiǎn	差一點	Adv.	almost	9
cháng	嘗	V	to taste; to try (food)	9
cháng	長	SV	long	7
chángcháng	常常	Adv.	often	2
Chángchéng	長城	PN	the Great Wall	7
Chángjiāng	長江	PN	Yangtze River	3
cháng yòng	常用	SV	commonly used	1
chǎo	*炒	V	to stir-fry; to fry	10
chē	車	N	vehicle; car	6
chéngle	成了	V	to become	8
chéngqiáng	城牆	N	city wall	7
chéngshì	城市	N	city	3
chéngwéi	成為	V	become	8
chéngyǔ	成語	N	idiom; set phrase	6
chī	吃	V	to eat	3
chīfàn	吃飯	VO	to eat (meal); to have meal	4

Pinyin	Character	Part of speech	Definition/function	Lesson no.
chóngzi	蟲子	N	insect	9
chūlái	出來	VP	to come out	5
chūshēng	出生	V	to be born	1
chúshī	廚師	N	cook; chef	10
Chǔguó	楚國	PN	one of the Warring States (770–256 B.C.)	6
chuán	傳	V	to pass on; to convey	7
chuāng	窗	N	window	7
chuántǒng	傳統	N	tradition	10
chūn	春	N	spring	1
cōng	*葱	N	scallion; onion	10
cōngming	聰明	SV	intelligent; bright	5
cóng	從	Prep.	from	3
cū	粗	SV	wide (in diameter); thick	8
cù	*醋	N	vinegar	10
dà	大	SV	big	2
dàjiā	大家	N	all of us; everyone	9
dàmǐ	大米	N	rice (uncooked rice)	3
dài	代	M	generation	2
dài	帶	V	to bring	6
dàn	蛋	N	egg	5
dāngrán	當然	Adv.	of course	6
dāng...shí	當……時	Conj.	when ...	7
dāngshí	當時	TW	then; at that time	7
dǎo	倒	V	to collapse; to fall	7
dào	到	V/CV	to arrive; to reach/to	4
dào	道	M	measure word for long and slender objects	7
dàolǐ	道理	N	reason	6
de	的	Pt.	marker (of noun modifier)	1
de	地	Pt.	adverbial marker	5
de	得	Pt.	verb complement marker	6
dé	得	V	to get; to obtain	9

Pinyin	Character	Part of speech	Definition/function	Lesson no.
dédào	得到	V	to get; to obtain; to gain	6
děi	得	MV	have to; must	9
děng	等	V	to wait	9
dī	低	SV/V	low; to lower	3
dírén	敵人	N	enemy	7
dì	第	Prefix	ordinal number prefix	4
dìdi	弟弟	N	younger brother	2
dìfang	地方	N	place; space	1
dìmíng	地名	N	place name	1
dìshang	地上	N	(on) the ground; on the earth	4
diànbào	電報	N	telegraph	7
diànhuà	電話	N	telephone	7
dōng	東	N.	east	3
dōngfāng	東方	N	the east	4
dōngtiān	冬天	N	winter	3
dōngxi	東西	N	thing; object	2
dǒng	懂	V	to understand; to comprehend	6
dòng	凍	V	to freeze	8
dòngwu	動物	N	animal	1
dōu	都	Adv.	all	1
dú	毒	N	poison	9
duì	對	SV	right	2
duì	對	CV	toward; to	6
duìbuqǐ	對不起	IE	I am sorry; Excuse me	1
duō	多	SV	many; much	1
éi	欸	Interj.	Hey!	6
ěrduo	耳朵	N	ear	8
èr	二	Nu.	two	2
fāxiàn	發現	V	to discover; to find	7
fānyì	翻譯	V/N	to translate; translation	8
fàn'guǎn	飯館	N	restaurant	10

Pinyin	Character	Part of speech	Definition/function	Lesson no.
fāngfǎ	方法	N	method; way; means	10
fángzi	房子	N	house	3
fàng	放	V	to put; to put in; to add	10
fēi	飛	V	to fly	4
fēicháng	非常	Adv.	extremely; unusually; extraordinarily	4
fēnkāi	分開	VP	separate; to part	5
fēng	風	N	wind	5
fú	扶	V	to support with the hand; to hold by the arm	7
fù	父	N	father	1
gānjìng	乾淨	SV	clean	5
gǎn	趕	V	to drive (a horse or a chariot)	6
gǎn	敢	MV	dare	8
gǎndòng	感動	V/SV	to move; to touch/ touched; moved	8
gǎnjī	感激	V	to feel grateful or indebted	8
gǎnxiè	感謝	V	to thank; to be grateful	9
gàn	幹	V	to do	8
gāng	剛	Adv.	moment ago; just	9
gāngcái	剛才	TW	just now; a moment ago	8
gāo	高	SV	high, tall	3
gāoxìng	高興	SV	happy; glad	1
gēge	哥哥	N	older brother	2
gè	個	M	general measure word	1
gè	各	Pron.	each; every	10
gěi	給	CV/V	for (for the benefit of); to; to give	2
gēn	跟	CV/V	with; and; follow	2
gēn	根	M	measure word for long and slender object	8
gōngzuò	工作	V/N	to work; work; job	3
gòu	够	SV/Adv.	enough	6
gǔ	古	SV	ancient	4
gǔlǎo	古老	SV	ancient	7
gùshì	故事	N.	story	6

Comprehensive Vocabulary List

Pinyin	Character	Part of speech	Definition/function	Lesson no.
guì	貴	SV	(honorific) your; expensive; costly	1
guìxìng	*貴姓	IE	your honorable surname	1
guójiā	國家	N	country	7
guǒpí	果皮	N	fruit skin	9
guò	過	V	to pass; to spend (time)	5
guòrìzi	過日子	VO	to live (one's life)	4
hái	孩	N	child	1
hái	還	Adv.	still, yet	2
hàn	汗	N	sweat; perspiration	5
hǎo	好	SV	good; well	1
hǎochù	好處	N	good; benefit; advantage	6
hǎokàn	好看	SV	pretty; good-looking	3
hǎoxiàng	好像	Adv.	as if; seemingly	6
hē	喝	V	to drink	6
hé	和	Conj.	and	2
hé	河	N	river	3
hēi	黑	SV	black; dark	5
hěn	很	Adv.	very; quite	1
héngxīn	恆心	N.	perseverance in)	8
hòu	厚	SV	thick	5
hòumian	後面	L/PW	back; behind; rear	1
hòutou	後頭	L/PW	behind	3
hú	湖	N	lake	3
Húnán	*湖南	PN	a province in China	10
hútu	糊塗	SV	muddled; confused; bewildered	6
hùxiāng	互相	Adv.	mutually, each other	2
huá	*華	N	flower; abbreviation for China	1
huà	畫	V/N	draw; paint/drawing, painting	6
huàirén	壞人	N	evildoer; scoundrel	8
huí	回	V	to return; to go back	4
huì	會	MV/V	will; would/ know how to...	4

Pinyin	Character	Part of speech	Definition/function	Lesson no.
huó	活	V	to live; to be alive	9
huòzhě	或者	Conj.	either . . . or . . . (in affirmative sentence); or	10
jǐ	幾	Nu./QW	several/how many	2
jí	急	SV	urgent; emergent	6
jíle	極了	IE	extremely	6
jì	季	N	season of the year	10
jìjié	季節	N	season of the year	4
jìxiàlái	記下來	VP	to take down; to record	9
jìxìng	記性	N	memory	8
jiātíng	家庭	N	family	2
jiāzhǎng	家長	N	the head of a family; patriarch	2
jiǎnzhí	簡直	Adv.	simply	6
jiàn	件	M	measure word for clothes or matters	2
jiàn	箭	N	arrow	4
jiàn	建	V	to build; to construct; to establish	7
jiàndào	見到	V	to see; to be able to see	4
jiànkāng	健康	N/SV	health; healthy	9
jiāng	姜	N	family name; ginger	9
jiǎngjiu	講究	SV/V	to be particular about; to stress; to strive for	10
jiāo	教	V	to teach	9
jiāoào	驕傲	SV	arrogant; proud	8
jiǎo	腳	N	foot	5
jiào	叫	V	to call; to name; to order; to shout	1
jiàoyù	教育	V/N	to educate; education	8
jiàozuò	叫做	V	to be called, to be known as	10
jiéhūn	結婚	VO	to marry	2
jiějie	姐姐	N	older sister	2
jièshào	介紹	V/N	to introduce; introduction	2
jìn	進	V	to enter; to advance	7
jìnbù	進步	V	to progress; to improve	8
jīngguò	經過	V	to pass through	3

Comprehensive Vocabulary List

Pinyin	Character	Part of speech	Definition/function	Lesson no.
jiǔ	九	Nu.	nine	2
jiǔ	久	SV	long (time)	5
jiǔ	酒	N	wine; alcohol; liquor	6
jiùhuó	救活	V	to save (a life)	8
jiùshì	就是	adv./VP	namely; to be no other than	4
juéde	覺得	V	to sense; to feel	4
juédìng	決定	V/N	to decide; decision	2
kànjiàn	看見	VP	see	4
kànshàngqù	看上去	VP	to seem; to appear	9
kē	棵	M	measure word for tree, etc.	3
kělián	可憐	SV	pitiful	8
kě'néng	可能	Adv./SV	probably; maybe; possible	1
kèrén	客人	N	guest	10
kěyǐ	可以	MV	may; can	2
kèkǔ	刻苦	SV	hardworking; painstaking	8
kòng	空	N	free time; spare time	10
kǒu	口	N/M	mouth; MW for member of a family	2
kū	哭	V	to cry; to weep	7
kuài	塊	M	unit of currency; piece	2
kuài	快	SV	fast; quick	6
kuàizi	筷子	N	chopsticks	10
kuān	寬	SV	wide	3
là	辣	SV	hot; peppery; spicy	10
làjiāo	*辣椒	N	hot pepper; chili	10
láiyuán	來源	N	origin; source	1
lǎo	老	SV	old	2
lǎodàye	老大爺	N	a respectful address term for elderly men	6
lǎohuà	老話	N	old saying	7
le	了	Pt.	indicates a change of state	2
léi	雷	N	thunder	5
lèi	累	SV	tired	3

Pinyin	Character	Part of speech	Definition/function	Lesson no.
lěng	冷	SV	cold	3
lí	離	CV	away from	6
Lǐ	李	N	a surname	1
lǐ	裏	Loc.	in; inside	2
lǐ	里	M	a Chinese unit of length (= 1/2 kilometer)	7
LǐShízhēn	*李時珍	PN	famous Chinese herbalist	9
lǐwù	禮物	N	gift; present	10
lìqi	力氣	N	physical strength; effort	4
lìshǐ	歷史	N	history	8
lián...dōu...	連...都...	IE	even . . .	6
liánjiē	連接	V	to link; to join	7
liǎng	兩	Nu.	two (used before a measure word)	2
liǎngbiān	兩邊	PW	both sides	3
liáo	聊	V	to chat	10
liǎobuqǐ	了不起	IE	excellent; amazing; remarkable	7
líng	零	Nu.	zero	2
lìngwài	另外	Conj.	in addition; besides	10
Liú	*劉	N	a surname	1
liú	流	V	to flow	3
liù	六	Nu.	six	2
lóu	樓	N	storied building; floor	3
lù	路	N	road	6
luóbo	*蘿卜	N	turnip; radish	10
ma	嗎	Interj.	yes/no question marker	1
ma	嘛	Pt.	particle	2
māma	媽媽	N	mother	2
mǎ	馬	N	horse; a surname	1
mǎchē	馬車	N	a chariot; a (horse-drawn) carriage	6
mǎshàng	馬上	Adv.	immediately	4
mǎi	買	V	to buy	2
Màidāngláo	*麥當勞	PN	McDonald's restaurant	10

Comprehensive Vocabulary List

Pinyin	Character	Part of speech	Definition/function	Lesson no.
màn	慢	SV	slow	5
máng	忙	SV	busy	2
méiguānxi	沒關係	IE	It doesn't matter; Never mind	1
méiyǒu	沒有	V	to have not; without	2
měi	每	Pron.	every	4
měi	美	SV/N	beautiful; pretty; abbreviation for America	1
měiguó	美國	PN	America	1
měiwèi	美味	N	delicious food; delicacy	10
mèimei	妹妹	N	younger sister	2
miàn	麵	N	flour	3
miàn	面	N/Loc.	side	3
mínzú	民族	N	nationality; ethnic group	10
míng	名	N	name; given name	1
míng	明	SV	bright; brilliant	1
míngtiān	明天	TW	tomorrow	2
míngzi	名字	N	given name; full name	1
mó	磨	V	to grind	8
mǔ	母	N	mother	1
nà/nèi	那	Pron.	that	1
nàlǐ	那裏	PW	there	3
nàme	那麼	Conj.	then; therefore	4
nǎinai	奶奶	N	grandmother	8
nán	男	SV	male (as modifier only)	1
nán	南	N	south	3
nánchī	難吃	SV	bad-tasting; distasteful	9
nánfāng	南方	N	the south	3
nánguò	難過	SV	sad; aggrieved	4
nǎr	哪兒	QW	where	3
nàr	那兒	PW	there	3
ne	呢	Pt.	follow-up question marker	1
néng	能	MV	can, to be able to	2

Pinyin	Character	Part of speech	Definition/function	Lesson no.
nǐ	你	Pron.	you	1
niánqīng	年輕	SV	young	6
nín	您	Pron.	(respectful, honorific) you	1
niú	牛	N	ox; cow; bull; a surname	1
nóngfū	農夫	N	peasant; farmer	8
nuǎnhuo	暖和	SV	warm	8
nǔlì	努力	V/SV/N	to make great efforts; to try hard	8
nǚ	女	SV	female (as modifier only)	1
nǚzǐ	女子	N	young woman	7
ō, ò	噢	Interj.	Oh!	1
pà	怕	V	to fear; to be afraid	4
pángǔ	盤古	N	the name of the god who, according to the legend, created the world	5
pángbiān	旁邊	PW	side	3
pǎo	跑	V	to run	6
péngyou	朋友	N	friend	2
pí	皮	N	skin	9
pǐnzhǒng	品種	N	breed, variety	10
píng	瓶	N/M	bottle	6
pò	破	V	to break; broken	5
pǔtōngrén	普通人	N	ordinary people; commoners	9
qī	七	Nu.	seven	2
qíguài	奇怪	SV	strange; surprising; odd	8
qǐ	起	Adv.	up	7
qì	氣	N	breath; air; gas	5
qìhòu	氣候	N	climate; weather	10
qiān	千	Nu.	thousand	2
qián	錢	N	money	2
qiánmian	前面	L/PW	the front; ahead; preceding	1
qiántou	前頭	L/PW	in the front	3
qiē	切	V	to cut; to slice	10

Pinyin	Character	Part of speech	Definition/function	Lesson no.
qīnyǎn	親眼	Adv.	(to see) with one's own eyes	7
qīnzì	親自	Adv.	personally; in person	9
qīng	輕	SV	light	5
qǐng	請	V	please; to invite	1
qǐngkè	請客	VO	to entertain guests; to give a dinner party	10
qǐngwèn	請問	IP	May I ask	1
qiū	秋	N	autumn	1
qiú	求	V	to beg; to pray for	9
qù	去	V	to go; to go to	4
qǔzi	曲子	N	tune; melody	6
ràng	讓	V	to let; to give away; to yield	10
rè	熱	SV	hot	3
rén	人	N	human being; person; people	1
rénmín	人民	N	the people	10
rènshi	認識	V	to know; to recognize; to be acquainted with	1
róngyi	容易	SV	easy	7
rúguǒ	如果	Conj.	if; in case	4
sān	三	Nu.	three	2
shān	山	N	mountain	3
Shāndōng	*山東	PN	a province of China	10
Shānxī	*山西	PN	a province in China	10
Shànghǎi	上海	PN	Shanghai	1
shàngshēng	上升	VP	to rise	5
shàngzuò	上座	N	seat for the guest of honor	10
shāohuǒ	燒火	VO	to make a fire; to light a fire	7
shǎo	少	SV	few	2
shào	少	SV	young	2
shé	蛇	N	snake; serpent	6
shè	射	V	to shoot	4
shèlì	設立	V	to set up; to establish	7
shéi/shuí	誰	QW	who; whom	2

Pinyin	Character	Part of speech	Definition/function	Lesson no.
shēn	深	SV	deep	8
shēntǐ	身體	N	body	5
shén	神	N	god; spiritual being	4
shénme	甚麼	QW	what	1
Shénnóng	神農	N	Chinese god of agriculture	9
shēngqì	生氣	V/SV	to get angry; to take offense; angry; upset	4
shēngrì	生日	N	birthday	2
shēngyīn	聲音	N	voice; sound	5
shī	詩	N	poetry; verse	8
shīrén	詩人	N	poet	8
shí	十	Nu.	ten	2
shíhou	時候	N	time	4
shíjiān	時間	N	time	1
shítou	石頭	N	stone; rock	8
shì	試	V	to try	9
shì	是	V	to be	1
shì	事	N	thing; matter	2
shìjiè	世界	N	the world	5
shìqing	事情	N	matter; event; thing; business	4
shǒudū	首都	N	capital	3
shǒuxiān...hòulái	首先...後來	conj.	first . . . then . . .	3
shū	書	N	book	3
shūcài	*蔬菜	N	vegetable	10
shūfu	舒服	SV	comfortable	4
shù	樹	N	tree	3
shùmù	樹木	N	tree	5
shùyè	樹葉	N	leaf	9
shuì	睡	V	to sleep	4
shuǐguǒ	水果	N	fruit	9
shuō	說	V	to speak	2
shuōmíng	說明	V	to illustrate; to show; to indicate	6

Pinyin	Character	Part of speech	Definition/function	Lesson no.
sǐ	死	V	to die	4
sì	四	Nu.	four	2
Sìchuān	*四川	PN	a province in China	10
sìzhōu	四周	PW	all around	7
suān	酸	SV	sour; tart	10
suàn	*蒜	N	garlic	10
suīrán	雖然	Adv.	although, though	6
suīrán...dànshi	雖然...但是...	Conj.	although; though	10
suì	歲	M	year (of age)	9
Sūn Sīmiǎo	*孫思邈	PN	famous Chinese herbalist	9
suǒyǐ	所以	Conj.	so; therefore	3
tā	它	Pron.	it	6
tàitai	太太	N	lady; Mrs.; wife	1
tàiyáng	太陽	N	sun	4
tánqín	彈琴	VO	to play the zither	6
táng	*糖	N	sugar	10
Tángcháo	唐朝	PN	Tang Dynasty	8
tèdiǎn	特點	N	characteristic; distinguishing feature	10
tī	踢	V	to kick	5
tì	替	CV/V	for (take the place of); to replace	2
tiān	天	N	sky; heaven, day	4
tiān	添	V	to add	6
tiānxìng	天性	N	natural instincts; nature	8
tián	甜	SV	sweet	10
tiáo	條	M	MW for river and long, narrow things	3
tiáoliào	*調料	N	condiment; seasoning	10
tiě	鐵	N	iron	8
tīnghuà	聽話	VO	to heed what an elder or superior says; to be obedient	2
tíng	停	V	to stop	6
tǒngyī	統一	V/SV	to unify; to unite; unified; united	7
tóu	頭	N/M	head/measure word for animals	6

Pinyin	Character	Part of speech	Definition/function	Lesson no.
tóufa	頭髮	N	hair	5
tǔdòu	*土豆	N	potato	10
tù	吐	V	to vomit	9
wài	外	Loc.	outside	3
wàiguórén	外國人	N	foreigner	7
wàiyǔ	外語	N	foreign language	8
wánquán	完全	Adv.	completely; entirely; absolutely	4
wǎnshang	晚上	N	evening	4
wàn	萬	Nu	ten thousand	7
Wáng	王	N	a surname	1
wàng	往	Prep.	toward	3
wàng	忘	V	to forget	8
wēixiǎn	危險	N/SV	danger; dangerous	9
wěi	*偉	SV	great	1
wěidà	偉大	SV	great; mighty	7
wèi	位	M	polite measure word for persons	1
wèi	為	CV	for	2
wèidao	味道	N	taste	9
wèile	為了	Prep.	for the sake of; in order to	7
wèishénme	為甚麼	QW	why	2
wēnhé	溫和	SV	mild, moderate	10
wén	聞	V	to smell	10
wénhuà	文化	N	culture	7
wénmíng	聞名	SV	famous; well-known	7
wèn	問	V	to ask	1
wèntí	問題	N	problem; question	2
wǒ	我	Pron.	I; me	1
wǔ	五	Nu.	five	2
xī	西	N	west	3
xīfāng	西方	N	the West	4
xīwàng	希望	V/N	to hope; to expect; expectation	1

Pinyin	Character	Part of speech	Definition/function	Lesson no.
xīyào	西藥	N	Western medicine	9
xíguàn	習慣	N	custom; habit	10
xì	細	SV	thin; slender	8
xià	下	Loc.	under	3
xiàchén	下沉	VP	to sink	5
xiàtiān	夏天	N	summer	3
xiàxuě	下雪	VO	to snow	3
xiàyǔ	下雨	VO	to rain	4
xiānsheng	先生	N	gentleman; Mr.; husband	1
xián	鹹	SV	salty	10
xiàndài	現代	N/SV	modern times; modern	2
xiànzài	現在	TW	now; at present	2
xiāngxìn	相信	V	to believe in; to have faith in	8
xiǎng	想	V/MV	to think; to miss; to want; would like to	2
xiàngzhēng	象徵	N/V	symbol; to symbolize	7
xiāoxi	消息	N	news	7
xiǎojie	小姐	N	Miss; young lady	1
xiǎokàn	小看	V	to despise; to look down upon	9
xiě, xuè,	血	N	blood	5
xiè (dùzi)	瀉(肚子)	V(O)	to have diarrhea	9
xīn	新	SV	new	5
xīnxiān	新鮮	SV	fresh; new	10
xíng	行	SV	okay	5
xíngzhuàng	形狀	N	shape; form	10
xīngqī	星期	N	week	10
xǐng	醒	V	to wake up; to be awake	5
xìng	姓	V/N	one's surname is; surname	1
xìngqu	興趣	N	interest	6
xiōngdì	兄弟	N	brothers	2
xiōngkǒu	胸口	N	chest	8
xiūxi	休息	V	to rest; to take a break	7

Pinyin	Character	Part of speech	Definition/function	Lesson no.
xǔduō	許多	Adv.	many	9
xué	學	V	to study; to learn	2
xuéxí	學習	V/N	to study; to learn	8
ya	呀	Pt.	soft tone marker	9
yān	烟	N	smoke	7
yán	*鹽	N	salt	10
yǎnjīng	眼睛	N	eye	5
yàng	樣	N	pattern	2
yào	要	V/MV	to need; to want; to be going to	2
yǎo	咬	V	to bite; to snap at	8
yàoburán	要不然	Conj.	otherwise	9
yàoshì	要是	Conj.	if	9
yéye	爺爺	N	grandfather	2
yě	也	Adv.	too; also; as well; either	1
yěxǔ	也許	Adv.	perhaps; maybe	9
yè	夜	N	night	7
yī	一	Nu	one	1
yīfu	衣服	N	clothes	7
yīshēng	醫生	N	doctor	9
yídìng	一定	SV/Adv.	certain; certainly; definitely	1
yígòng	一共	Adv.	altogether	2
yíkuàir	一塊兒	Adv.	together	4
yíyàng	一樣	SV	the same	3
yǐhòu	以後	TW	after	2
yǐjīng	已經	Adv.	already	2
yǐqián	以前	TW	before; formerly; previously	1
yì	*億	Nu.	hundred million	2
Yì	羿	N	the name of the god who, according to the legend, shot down nine suns	4
yìdiǎnr	一點兒	IE	a little	6
yìqǐ	一起	Adv.	together	2

Pinyin	Character	Part of speech	Definition/function	Lesson no.
yìsi	意思	N	meaning	1
yìxiē	一些	Pron.	some	2
yīnwèi	因為	Conj.	because; because of; due to	3
yīnyuè	音樂	N	music	6
yīnyuèjiā	音樂家	N	musician	6
yǐnshí	飲食	N	food and drink; diet	10
yīng	英	N	blossom; abbreviation for England	1
yīnggāi	應該	MV	should; ought to	2
yīngwén	英文	N	English	2
yòng	用	V/CV	to use; with; by means of	2
yǒu	有	V	to have; to exist; there is/are	1
yǒude	有的	Pron.	some	1
yǒuxiào	有效	SV	effective	9
yǒuyìsi	有意思	SV	interesting	4
yǒuyòng	有用	SV	useful; effective	7
yòu	右	N/Loc.	right	3
yòu	又	Adv.	again	5
yú	魚	N	fish	3
yuǎn	遠	SV	far; distant	6
yuè...yuè...	越...越...	Conj.	the more . . . the more	6
yuèláiyuè	越來越	Adv.	more and more	8
yuèliang	月亮	N	moon	5
yún	雲	N	cloud	5
zài	在	CV	at; on; in	2
zàijiàn	再見	IE	Good-bye	1
zěnmēyàng	怎麼樣	IE	How are things? How about . . . ?	5
zhá	*炸	V	to deep fry	10
zhǎi	窄	SV	narrow	3
zhànzhe	站著	V	to be standing	5
Zhāng	張	N	a surname	1
zhǎngde	長得	V	to grow up to look; look	4

Pinyin	Character	Part of speech	Definition/function	Lesson no.
zhàngfu	丈夫	N	husband	7
zháojí	着急	SV/V	worried; to feel anxious; to worry	2
zhǎodào	找到	VP	to find	7
Zhào	*趙	N	a surname	1
zhàogù	照顧	V	to look after	2
zhàoxiàng	照相	VO	to take pictures; to photograph	7
zhe	着	suffix	verb suffix indicating durative state	5
zhè/zhèi	這	Pron.	this	1
zhèxiē	這些	Pron.	these	2
zhèyàng	這樣	IE	in this way	7
zhēn	真	Adv.	really; truly	3
zhēn	針	N	needle	8
zhēng	*蒸	V	to steam	10
zhēngkāi	睜開	VP	to open (one's eyes)	5
zhèr	這兒	PW	here	2
zhīdào	知道	V	to know; to realize; to be aware of	4
zhīshi	知識	N	knowledge	8
zhǐ	只	Adv.	only	2
zhìbìng	治病	VO	to treat a disease	9
zhōngguó	中國	PN	China	1
zhōngjiān	中間	PW	middle	3
zhōngyào	中藥	N	Chinese herbal medicine	9
zhǒng	種	N/M	kind; sort; type	7
zhòng	重	SV	heavy	5
zhòngdì	種地	VO	to farm; to cultivate the land	9
zhòngshì	重視	V	to pay attention; to take something seriously	10
zhòngyào	重要	SV	important	10
Zhōu	周	N	a surname	1
zhǔ	*煮	V	to boil; to cook	10
zhǔrén	主人	N	host	10
zhǔshí	主食	N	staple food; principal food	10

Pinyin	Character	Part of speech	Definition/function	Lesson no.
zhǔyào	主要	SV	main; major	10
zhǔyi	主意	N	idea	2
zhù	住	V	to live	2
zhù	築	V	to build; to construct	7
zhuā	抓	V	to force to go; to arrest	7
zhǔnbèi	準備	V/N	to prepare; to get ready; preparation	10
zìjǐ	自己	Pron.	self	2
zǒng	總	Adv.	sooner or later; eventually	8
zǒngdeláishuō	總的來說	IE	generally speaking	10
zǒngsuàn	總算	Adv.	finally; at last	4
zú	足	N	foot	6
zuì	最	Adv.	most (used to form superlative)	3
zuìhòu	最後	Adv.	finally; the last	4
zuìjìn	最近	TW	recent	5
zuótiān	昨天	TW	yesterday	4
zuǒ	左	N/Loc.	left	3
zuò	做	V	to do	2
zuò	坐	V	to sit	7
zuòwèi	座位	N	seat; place	10

Appendix III
CHARACTER STROKE ORDER

第一課單字筆順表

中	國	人	的
姓	名	前	面
是	後	很	多
常	用	有	百
個	都	來	源

第一課單字筆順表

比	方	說	以
前	地	動	物
字	定	意	思
父	母	希	望
男	女	孩	出

第一課單字筆順表

生	地	北	京
可	能	也	時
問	您	好	請
問	貴	我	呢
吧	先	小	姐

第一課單字筆順表

甚	麼	上	海
這	太	高	興
認	識	你	嗎
不	那	位	噢
對	起	沒	關

第一課單字筆順表

係	再見	見	張
李	王	劉	趙
周	馬	牛	明
偉	美	英	華
春	秋		

第二課單字筆順表

家	庭	幾	代
十	住	在	起
老	少	口	長
聽	話	裏	後
照	顧	兄	弟

第二課單字筆順表

妹	互	相	幫
助	些	題	常
跟	決	自	己
應	該	誰	結
婚	還	只	想

第二課單字筆順表

要	現	已	經
為	事	件	說
替	主	明	天
日	給	買	東
西	錢	用	朋

第二課單字筆順表

友	介	紹	英
文	學	嘛	

第三課單字筆順表

大	高	山	河
最	條	部	江
南	邊	方	夏
熱	下	雨	那
湖	樹	愛	魚

第三課單字筆順表

和	米	雪	冷
因	所	面	從
低	往	流	窄
寬	兩	過	城
市	首	房	子

第三課單字筆順表

左	右	真	啊
外	頭	旁	棵
工	作	累	哪
兒			

第四課單字筆順表

陽	早	得	完
全	每	到	去
開	始	飛	直
回	就	所	知
道	共	覺	塊

第四課單字筆順表

想	看	見	會
非	變	死	件
情	神	馬	氣
力	射	箭	羿
難	拿	才	玩

第四課單字筆順表

舒	服	故	

第五課單字筆順表

久	蛋	盤	古
睡	醒	眼	睛
睜	黑	手	腳
身	體	踢	打
出	輕	重	乾

第五課單字筆順表

淨	慢	昇	成
沉	分	站	着
厚	又	風	雲
聲	音	雷	髮
月	亮	新	世

第五課單字筆順表

界	聰	麼	喜
歡	季	節	花
風			

第六課單字筆順表

成	語	則	對
彈	琴	樂	得
頭	它	曲	像
趣	畫	蛇	添
足	喝	酒	瓶

第六課單字筆順表

當	然	夠	快
馬	本	連	雖
到	必	處	年
輕	趕	車	急
楚	停	繁	帶

第六課單字筆順表

第	極	跑	哎
呀	簡	糊	塗
道	理	越	

第七課單字筆順表

萬	四	里	休
牆	周	聞	建
保	護	秦	始
皇	統	起	接
孟	姜	抓	丈

第七課單字筆順表

夫	這	樣	設
立	發	燒	敵
消	息	傳	電
衣	哭	倒	古
化	象	徵	報

第七課單字筆順表

辦	法	歷	史
夜	雄	偉	總
算	親	扶	

第八課單字筆順表

詩	習	忘	奶
努	力	河	鐵
棒	石	磨	奇
怪	針	敢	相
信	粗	把	細

第八課單字筆順表

朵	感	步	終
於	為	恆	扔
幹	耳		

第九課單字筆順表

藥	根	葉	果
皮	蟲	許	治
病	試	佑	先
姜	種	親	當
毒	瀉	羞	點

第九課單字筆順表

健	康	危	險
普	遍	謝	記
效	呀	錯	活
味			

第十課單字筆順表

氣	候	飲	食
習	慣	溫	新
鮮	品	民	麵
蔬	講	究	菜
各	另	甜	鹹

第十課單字筆順表

準	備	廚	辣
或	者	空	聊
禮	酸	切	季
形	狀	方	禮
客	管	鬥	族

第十課單字筆順表

讓	但	筷	視
座	按	作	